WILD
swimming
Croatia &
Slovenia

Discover the most beautiful springs,
rivers, waterfalls, lakes and beaches in
Croatia and Slovenia

Hansjörg Ransmayr

WILD
THINGS
PUBLISHING

CONTENTS

THE SWIMMING SPOTS

The north of Slovenia

01 Mežica
02 Učja
03 Nadiža
04 Globoški Potok waterfall
05 Sušec waterfalls
06 Kozjak waterfall
07 Krampež waterfall
08 Kanal ob Soči
09 Soča, Lepena
10 Šunikov water park
11 Most na Soči reservoir
12 Upper reaches of the Idricja
13 Bača pri Modreju
14 Source of the Soča
15 Savica waterfall
16 Lake Bohinj
17 Wocheiner Save bei Polje
18 Gremčica waterfall
19 Wocheiner Save Nomenj
20 Lake Bled (Blejsko jezero)
21 Radovna
22 Wocheiner Save at Radovljica
23 Dovžan gorge
24 Lomščica waterfall
25 Stegovnik waterfall
26 Kokra valley
27 Ank waterfall
28 Lake Planšarsko
29 Rinka waterfall
30 Repov waterfall
31 Savinja
32 Lake Smartno
33 Lake Blaguš

The south of Slovenia

34 Strunjan moon cove
35 Debeli Rtič
36 Vipava
37 Bela
38 Planina cave
39 Unica
40 Škocjan "fairy pool"
41 Lake Cerknica

42 Ljubljanica
43 Lake Podpeško
44 Krka at Žužemberk
45 Kočevje mining lake
46 Krupa
47 Kolpa/Podzemlj
48 Kolpa/Otok
49 Kolpa/Griblje
50 Kolpa/Domačija Kuzma
51 Kolpa/Adlešiči

Istria and the north of Croatia

52 Butori waterfall
53 Buzet waterfall trail
54 Kotli
55 Zarečki Krov waterfall
56 Gologorički waterfall
57 Sopot waterfall
58 The Blue Eye by the Raša
59 Sentonina staza
60 Saccorgiarna cove
61 Cape Kamenjak
62 Havišće beach
63 Lake Lepenica
64 Zeleni Vir
65 Korana city beach
66 Brisalo waterfall
67 Lake Jarun
68 Lake See

Central Croatia

69 Javna beach
70 Mrežnica
71 Korana, Rastoke
72 Slunjčica
73 Lopar peninsula
74 Lukovo
75 Pudarica beach
76 Zavratnica
77 Tovarnele
78 Olib
79 Gospa od Zečeva
80 Paklenica gorge

81 Berberov Buk
82 Zrmanja entry point
83 Krupa
84 Dugi Otok
85 Karišnica
86 Lake Vrana
87 Krčić waterfall
88 Krčić valley
89 Source of the Cetina
90 Lake Peruća
91 Lake Torak
92 Source of the Čikola

The south of Croatia

93 Šibenik submarine bunker
94 Veliko jezero/Šibenik
95 Grab
96 Ruda
97 Dragon Eye's Lake (Zmajevo oko)
98 Stružica
99 Blato on Cetina
100 Dva Oka
101 Nugal beach
102 Blue Lake
103 Baćina Lakes
104 "Blue Eye" of Desne
105 Duba cove
106 Pijavičino cove
107 Vučine cove
108 Veliko jezero/Mljet
109 Sutmholjska beach
110 Odysseus's Cave
111 Mala Saplunara cove
112 Brana
113 Šunj
114 Koločep island
115 Zaton
116 Ombla
117 Dubrovniks beaches by the city walls
118 Lokrum
119 Kupari cove
120 Pasjača beach

FROM MOUNTAINS TO
MEDITERRANEAN

INTRODUCTION

From alpine to Mediterranean habitats, Croatia and Slovenia are made for wild swimming. From the idyllic to the adventurous, from fresh water to brackish and salt water, there is a fabulous range of swimming possibilities. Added to that, and more than being merely a pleasant bonus, there is spectacular cultural and culinary choice on offer, from tiny mountain chapels to mighty citadels, from the Bled *kremšnita* (a special cream slice) to *brodet*, a frog and eel casserole typical of the river Neretva. Even wine aficionados will find that both countries cater for all palates. Slovenia is predominantly known for white wines such as Chardonnay, Sauvignon Blanc, Pinot Gris, Rébula and Malvasia, as well as the traditional red wine Teran, much appreciated by those in the know. In Istria, wine varieties such as Malvazija Istarska and Merlot are grown, whereas continental Croatia is dominated by Riesling and Graševina. In Dalmatia, the heavy red Dingač has gained a worldwide reputation.

Travelling as an explorer requires a certain degree of healthy curiosity as well as a readiness to step off the beaten track. However, those who are willing to face the unknown as wild swimming enthusiasts will reap rich rewards in both countries, gaining a wealth of new experiences and realisations. For example, Slovenia does not just comprise the Julian Alps and the cold river Soča but also breathtaking coves and bays and countless family-friendly bathing sites along its riverbanks, where the water is both pleasantly warm and clean. Wild-swimming travellers will also realise that Croatia has much more to offer than romantic islands and magnificent rocky beaches. It is home to vast primaeval forests and woodlands with secret ponds, as well as steppe lakes with unique fauna and flora and upland plateaus of karst rock where one can unexpectedly come across "blue eye" tarns.

In fact, Croatia and Slovenia present such a large number of potential wild-swimming spots that, as an author, I am spoilt for choice. However, my objective was not to compile a complete listing of every single body of water in these two countries but rather to provide a colourful and informative guide for current and future wild-swimming enthusiasts. I am well aware that there are many more spots to discover that are not included in this guide. Therefore, I like to regard my book primarily as a source of inspiration to practice wild swimming with body, mind and soul – as a "gentle art of swimming" with awe and respect for nature – as well as to actively protect the environment and all kinds of bodies of water, rather than exploiting them for humanity's ever-increasing need for resources. I also hope it serves as a reminder to always remain curious and open and to enjoy life. I certainly will adhere to these principles and hope that you will enjoy reading about the natural beauty of Croatia and Slovenia!

RESPECT &
RESPONSIBILITY

Water, H$_2$O, is the only chemical compound on earth that is naturally prevalent as a gas, solid and liquid. The latter state of matter, commonly referred to as "water", is what we are going to deal with in this guide. All readers who are interested in this element may appreciate the following information about how to enjoy water safely:

ASK...

... **local people on site** about swimming spots and their immediate environment. Are there any prohibitions, bans, hazards or tips?

RESPECT...

... **all bans on swimming**, as well as protected areas and breeding and spawning sites.
... **the environment**. Do not leave anything behind and don't use sun lotion when in the water.
... **the interests** of other people, whether they be anglers, paddlers or photographers.
... **your own limits**, resisting peer pressure if needed.

ALWAYS WATCH OUT FOR...

... **your children** by the waterside, even if they are wearing swimming or flotation aids.
... **those members of a group** who are the least fit on long hikes or swimming/paddling tours.
... **the weather** and the water and how they might develop or react.

ACCESSORIES

SWACK – a combination of a hiking backpack and a swim buoy that you can purchase from me. This smart piece of equipment does not just allow you to carry your luggage across the water, including mobile phone, camera and car key, but also provides sufficient buoyancy in an emergency to effortlessly keep you afloat. Due to its high-visibility colour, the SWACK also ensures that boat crews will see you much more easily.

PACKRAFTS – lightweight, compact backpack boats that allow for combined swimming and rafting tours. See also p. 314.

WILD SWIMMING PONCHOS – available in a lighter summer and warming winter version. The sleeveless ponchos are significantly lighter and quicker to put on than thermal tops and coats, especially when one is wet or when it is cold. They are also useful as a cover when changing clothes, especially in urban areas.

SWIM/AQUA SHOES – essential for dealing with the sharp-edged stones, broken glass or other rubbish that in certain places can make entering the water more dangerous than the swimming! For more demanding trips and canyon exploration, more robust canyoning shoes with non-slip Vibram soles are recommended.

THERMOS FLASK WITH GINGER TEA – just what you need to warm up quickly after a prolonged stay in cold water. Make sure that the ginger tea is hot. Just take pieces of ginger, pour hot water over them, and add lemon and honey if preferred. Alcohol, on the other hand, is absolutely counter-productive!

BICYCLE – highly recommended, especially for covering the "last mile" to your destination. In this way, you can leave the car off-site and avoid possible parking fees. Also, on the bank of large bodies of water, a bicycle makes searching for the best entry point much easier.

HOW TO FIND YOUR DESTINATION

THIS IS HOW THE GLOBAL POSITIONING SYSTEM (GPS) WORKS

Hundreds of satellites orbit the earth, continuously reporting their position and providing highly precise time details. When a GPS receiver is in contact with at least four satellites, it can use this data to calculate its position. This calculation will be more precise the more satellites the GPS is able to receive.

(NOT) A QUESTION OF FORMAT

GPS coordinates can be received, recorded and communicated in various formats.

In the northern hemisphere, the north value is always indicated first, followed by the east value. This book uses the decimal format, which can be converted into other formats at any time using software tools that are available online.

WHAT DO THE COORDINATES REFERENCE?

The coordinates in this book are not necessarily precise
to the last metre, but in essence they refer to the
entry point of the bathing or swimming spot – that is,
mostly to the point where the majority of the swimming
photographs were taken. The routing function can be
used to navigate to this spot.

GOOGLE MAPS IS YOUR SOLUTION

Of course, there are many highly specialised solutions
for digital tour planning and routing. However, in general,
Google Maps, which is freely available, is perfectly
sufficient for the task. Simply enter the GPS coordinates
on the computer or smart device and let the routing
function guide you to the spot, if needed. You can select
routing for whichever way you are travelling, be it by car,
public transport, bicycle or foot.

GOOGLE MAPS IS ALSO USEFUL OFFLINE

If you are concerned about the availability of an Internet
connection at your destination, it is sensible to download
and save the necessary map tiles at home. This means
that you have these map sections available offline on-
site, such as on your smartphone, so that you can use
them to navigate the terrain straightaway. Occasionally,
it can be useful to print the map sections at home, ideally
laminate them, and carry them with you in your backpack.

TYPES OF SWIM
SPRINGS, CAVES, WATERFALLS, MILLS AND COVES

SPRINGS

Springs and source-fed pools have fascinated humans since prehistoric times. Almost all ancient cultures had great reverence for spring deities. Frequently, springs are the preferred abodes of water spirits, fairies and nymphs. Many springs are believed to have healing properties. Even if these are often not recognised by conventional medicine, springs are most certainly sacred sites. In alpine regions, springs commonly manifest as tiny rills whose actual origin can hardly be traced. Only after confluence from other small streams do they eventually grow into more serious bodies of water. In Slovenia and Croatia, due to the karst rock, there are also other, entirely different phenomena: spring-fed pools where crystal-clear, icy-cold water surfaces in magnificent quantities. There is an old saying that "water is best at the source". In this sense, bathing in these "blue eyes" is an unforgettably sensual experience that leaves one feeling totally energised and rejuvenated.

CAVES

What is said about springs is also true for caves. They are frequently connected to legends and myths. This applies, in particular, if they carry water or conceal internal springs, which can often be the case in karst regions. It must be said, however, that not everybody is keen on the idea of swimming underground, especially if they can easily feel claustrophobic. In any case, cave swimming requires a certain effort, preparation and equipment, and such an undertaking should never be made on one's own. If artificial light is needed, always make sure that you have sufficient spare capacity: at least one backup light, and preferably two. For long swimming trips underground, it is recommended to have a safety boat at hand. So-called "packrafts" are ideally suited for this purpose because of their low packing weight or volume, and experienced cave divers swear by them.

Of course, you don't need natural caves for swimming underground. In Slovenia, it is possible to swim in a flooded mine (1). Croatia even offers the possibility of swimming in a few disused submarine bunkers (84, 92). Provided that such trips are well organised and guided, this kind of swimming can give you a real kick!

MILLS

Mills were the first "hydropower stations" invented by man, and from a design perspective they are ingenious. Much loved by romantics, mills are also great spots for wild swimming because, along many rivers, watermills and their infrastructure provide the ideal environment. The best example is the river Kolpa, whose most beautiful swimming spots are mainly located around mills. Early on in the history of watermills, people used to construct weirs by piling stones across the river. This technique allowed millers to utilise a constant water volume. At some mills, the outflowing leat is perfect for swimming. And because these leats are not normally deep, children are usually safe to play and swim here.

WATERFALLS

Some waterfall plunge pools are so small that they are just big enough for a dip, whereas others are suitable for proper swimming. What can be said of all of them is that they are definitely invigorating. Depending on the might and volume of the falling water, it is possible to get close to or even underneath the cascade and enjoy a massage from above and below. It should be pointed out that, for your initial tries, a certain eye and feeling for water, and the necessary experience (or even better a coach), are required. Sadly, from autumn 2020, Skradinski buk waterfall, one of the most popular and spectacular bathing spots in Croatia's Krka National Park, has been banned for public use. This is something that, sooner or later, might be on the cards for other much-loved waterfalls as well. Therefore, always ask about the current situation on-site. Sometimes it is just not possible to enjoy a swim, but waterfalls are still always worth a visit.

BEACHES

Croatia, in particular, has countless extremely well-known beaches, and both countries still provide "hidden beaches" that do not draw large crowds. Tightly packed and crowded beaches are normally the "convenience beaches" – those that are easy to access and also have certain facilities. If one is prepared to walk along the coast or explore it by boat, it is quite possible to discover secluded coves and beaches for oneself. A mountain bike can often be useful on these kinds of exploration trips. Remember to take a heavy-duty bicycle lock because, along steep coastlines in particular, it is often necessary to leave your bike at the top of the cliffs. Packrafts have also proven their worth on these "hybrid" trips (combinations of hiking, biking and swimming tours). When the sea is calm but the swimming distance is too great, or you want to take more luggage, packrafts even allow island hopping.

STREAMS AND RIVERS

THE SEA

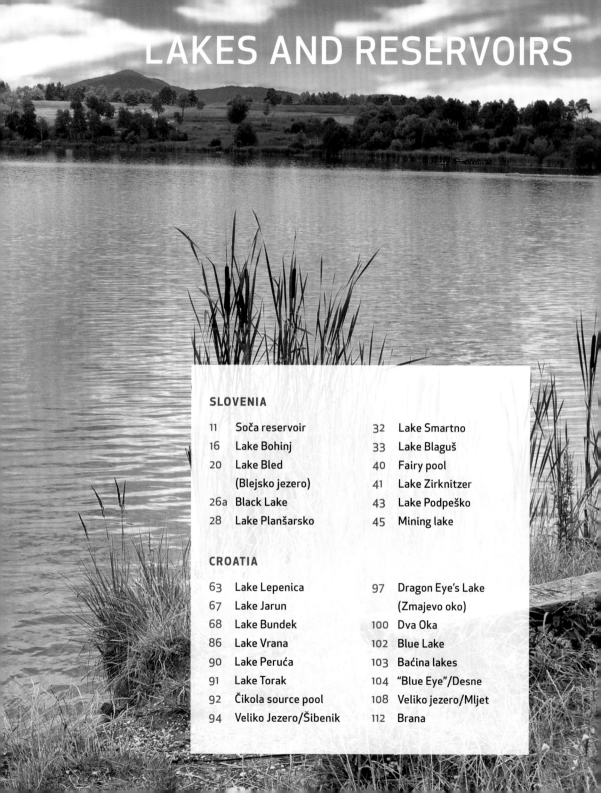

LAKES AND RESERVOIRS

SPRINGS

UNDERGROUND

THE FIVE MOST UNUSUAL SPOTS

THE FIVE MOST REMOTE SPOTS

THE FIVE MOST PHOTOGENIC SPOTS

THE FIVE MOST URBAN SPOTS

IF WE WERE GOING TO DISSOLVE NOW,
WE WOULD BE MORE THAN WE HAVE EVER BEEN

(Die Toten Hosen, a German punk-rock band)

SLOVENIA

A DECLARATION OF LOVE TO A SMALL BUT FANTASTIC COUNTRY

"I FEEL SLOVENIA" is the fitting slogan used by the Slovenian Tourist Board. It is a statement that everyone would likely agree with, including ambitious outdoor swimmers. The huge variety of landscapes, sceneries and bodies of water, as well as the low population density and large extended forests, are big attractions for nature lovers. Slovenia is very conscious of the natural gems that the country has to offer, and it is keen to preserve them as best it can. This is demonstrated by the fact that this country, which is the wealthiest among the countries of the former multi-ethnic state of Yugoslavia, has declared 36 per cent of its geographical area as "Natura 2000 Area" – that is, land worthy of protection. In contrast, only 15 per cent of Germany's and Austria's land surface have the same protection.

20,000km² of land surface may not sound much for a holiday destination, but it is precisely this size and the resulting small distances between the individual spots that make Slovenia a great experience, and not just for wild swimmers.

THE NORTH
OF SLOVENIA

This chapter comprises all of the spots to the north of the capital Ljubljana, described in order from west to east and from north to south.

While the north-west of the country features the high mountain ranges of the Julian Alps, Kara-wanks and Kamnik Alps, the north-east is cha-racterised by undulating uplands that eventually become the Pannonian Plain. Naturally, the different types of landscape are crossed by a variety of waterbodies. In the north-west, we find many waterfalls, mountain streams and tarns; whereas the north-east is dominated by wider rivers as well as steppe and forest lakes. The karst rock in the centre of the country produces its very own phenomena. So much can be said already; all of them have their own unique charm!

The north of Slovenia

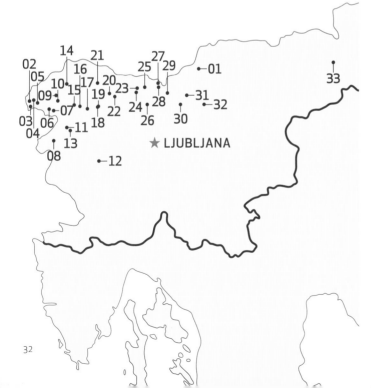

01

TUNNEL SWIMMING –
Mežica

The Petzen (Peca) mountain range is in the Karawanks on the Austrian–Slovenian border and has been known for its rich ore deposits since ancient times. On the Slovenian side of the border, Mežica had been a mining centre for more than 300 years. A total of 19 million tons of lead and zinc ore were extracted and almost 1,000km of tunnels were dug to achieve this task. When mining operations were abandoned more than 20 years ago, due to unprofitability, it also meant that the water drainage pumps were decommissioned. As a result, large tunnel sections are now underwater but are navigable with kayaks. Today, I run guided tours here, making it possible to swim in certain sections of the tunnel system.

To reach the site, board the miners' train and enter the mountain on a 15-minute journey. Clothes can be changed in a disused cavern, and you can wear a wetsuit if you wish. While hardened wild swimmers are likely to decline this offer, others may well regard this a welcome option, because the crystal-clear water is a freezing 8°C. For safety reasons, all swimmers carry a swim buoy as well as lighting. In addition, there is always a boat nearby to assist if needed. Afterwards, you can enjoy a hearty miners' snack underground. Then, following a brief and interesting ascent through the old tunnels, you will finally return to see the light of day.

→ **Directions:**
Either on the Slovenian side along the Meža valley, via Prevalje or Črna, or from Austria via Bleiburg.

→ **GPS:** 46.51242, 14.85735

PADDLING CLOSE TO THE BORDER –
Učja

In the western Julian Alps, on Monte Musi, is the source of the river Učja. This area is known as the region with the highest rainfall in Italy, which is why this wild mountain stream normally carries a good amount of water, even in summer. On its way east, 8km from its source, the river crosses the Slovenian border near the village of Uccea.

Alongside the river's upper reaches, on the left bank, is a small area of mountain pasture. Here, the Učja is still relatively slow-flowing and reasonably easy to reach from the road. A little further downstream, the river enters a narrow and inaccessible canyon until finally joining the river Soča at the village of Žaga. From this point in the valley you can take a spectacular and scenic mountain road across the Sedlo Učja to some beautiful pools that, in contrast to the river's lower reaches, are open and sunny.

→ **Directions:**
Coming from the Soča valley, at Žaga take the turning towards Italy and drive uphill towards the pass until you reach the last road bridge before the abandoned border post. The most beautiful bathing spot is approx. 200m downstream of the bridge.

→ **GPS:** 46.30589, 13.4188

PURE ROMANTICISM –
Nadiža

The Bela (white) Nadiža is one of two headwaters of this river that forms the border with Italy and is called Natisone in Italian. Near the small village of Breginj, the crystal-clear mountain stream (which is significantly warmer than the river Soča) is spanned by the so-called Napoleon's Bridge. Master masons from the village of Cembola in the Julian Veneto are said to have constructed the bridge around 1812. Like many similar bridges in the region, it carries Napoleon's name in memory of the French emperor's campaigns in that era.

From mid-June to the end of August, you need to pay a parking fee at this extremely romantic and popular bathing spot by the Nadiža (as one also has to at the other bathing sites on that river). But there is another option. You can choose a stress-free journey for a small fee from Kobarid and take the recommended hop-on-hop-off bus. It also stops at the Nadiža bathing spot at Robič, which is more suitable for families with small children.

→ **Directions:**
From Kobarid, follow Route 102 towards Italy until you reach the roundabout at Staro Selo. Take the second turning to the right and drive via Podbela towards Logje until you get to the small car park ahead of the bridge.

→ **GPS:** 46.229, 13.43898

SMALL POOL, GREAT SCENERY –
Globoški Potok waterfall

For hundreds of years, local farmers used ropes, which they stretched across the Učja canyon, to transport the hay from the inaccessible mountain pastures down to the valley. Today, six steel wires, 250m to 400m long, span the canyon, forming Europe's longest zip wire and offering unforgettable rides downhill. In theory, one could use this aid as a shortcut to the impressive waterfalls of Globoški Potok. In reality, however, you are likely to choose the hiking trail that leads uphill from the village of Žaga. Starting at the inn and following the signs, after approx. 20 minutes you approach a big mountain meadow with three stone huts and a well. Passing one of the arrival points of the zip wires, the trail leads slightly downhill to an inviting but relatively small plunge pool of the lowest of the Globoški Potok waterfalls. If you opt for returning via the more difficult trail through the lower section of the canyon, you will be rewarded with the possibility of enjoying the other pools of the Učja.

→ **Directions:**
In the Soča valley, coming from Kobarid, cross the Učja bridge. Immediately afterwards, at the Pri Mostu inn, turn off the road and park. If you are coming from Bovec, park on the left-hand side of the road ahead of the bridge or at the inn.

→ **GPS:** 46.31124, 13.46182

IDEAL FOR A QUICK DIP OR FOR CANYONING –
Sušec waterfalls

Waterfall bathing can hardly be less compli-cated. The plunge pool of the lowest Sušec waterfall is a real "convenience spot", which is why it can be very crowded during peak season. This is due less to the wild swimmers than to the canyoning groups run by local sports and adventure businesses. The attraction is understanda-ble. Over eons of time, the Sušec, which at this point is still a stream, has carved a picturesque miniature gorge into the northern slopes of the Stol mountains, including numerous pools, waterfalls, sliding gullies and abseiling sites.

For an effortless quick dip into the lowest pool, shower sandals are on this occasion sufficient, as it is very easy to get to the water. After your dip, you may be able to watch the canyoning groups during their abseiling practice, as well as jumping and sliding down the gullies.

→ **Directions:**
From the Bovec–Kobarid main road, near the village of Žaga and opposite the kayak entry point at Srpenica I, take the turning to an approx. 300m-long gravel track to the car park.

→ **GPS:** 46.2953, 13.48922

A SPECTACLE OF NATURE
IN A HISTORIC ENVIRONMENT –

Kozjak waterfall

Kobarid in the centre part of the Soča valley is not just the unsung pleasure capital of Slovenia but has equal importance as a museum city. The house, which is dedicated to the military history of World War I, has won several awards for being one of the best museums in Europe. You can get a sense of the traumatic history of the Battles of the Isonzo nearby. Start your trip at the car park (chargeable during peak season) and head for the Kozjak waterfall. After crossing a meadow, take the path uphill to your right. Trenches, artillery positions and bunker systems are silent witnesses to the former frontline.

Soon the trail descends into the valley that was formed by the Kozjak stream and features a total of six waterfalls. The first and smaller of the two easily accessible waterfalls appears below a small stone bridge on the way to the main fall. From here onwards, the scenery becomes even more breathtaking. Crossing small stone bridges and following paths enhanced with wooden planks, you walk through a small primaeval woodland and will soon hear the rushing of the waterfall. Now the gorge becomes even narrower and, passing along a safety rope, you reach the tiny viewing platform in the fascinating semi-cave, into which the 15m fall cascades from above.

Please note: A tourism website recently discouraged people from bathing in the plunge pool. Sooner or later, a bathing ban might be imposed – at least during peak season. I have also mentioned such a possibility concerning the beautiful Virje waterfall in Bovec.

→ **Directions:**
From Kobarid, cross Napoleon's Bridge (direction Drežnica) and use the car park to the right of the road. The walk from the car park to the waterfall takes half an hour.

→ **GPS:** 46.26066, 13.59053

PERFECT FOR FUN AND GAMES IN THE WATER –

Krampež waterfall

In the heat of the summer, adults will welcome the plunge pool of the lower Krampež fall as a great place for cooling off. For children, the relatively shallow and easily monitored pool is wonderful for playing in the water. The cascading waters also lend themselves as a natural shower, turning the location into a family-friendly photo opportunity.

Not suitable for children, the slippery and steep ascent to the upper pool is only partially secured with a brittle rope. The upper pool is even smaller than the lower one but attracts considerably fewer visitors and offers pretty views of the valley.

→ **Directions:**
From Kobarid, drive over Napoleon's Bridge and uphill to Drežnica, then take a right turn towards Koseč. Just outside Drežnica, on the left, is an information board about the waterfall trail. Park on the side of the road and follow the signs. The hike to the lower Krampež fall takes 15 minutes.

→ **GPS:** 46.25677, 13.62455

Lower fall pool

Upper fall

POPULAR FOR ITS DIVING EVENT –
Kanal ob Soči

This picturesque village on the river Soča is situated in the Primorska region between Tolmin and Nova Gorica. Here, the influence of the milder Mediterranean climate can be both felt and seen. Botanical proof comes in the form of imposing fig trees and cypresses.

The plunge pool gorges, which have been carved into the rocks by the river Soča, are up to 10m deep. This is the reason why, apart from a beautiful village beach, there is ample opportunity for cliff-diving. Truly spectacular are the dives during the annual bridge-diving event, for which a special platform has been constructed. This event normally takes place on the first weekend in August. It attracts thousands of onlookers and is best viewed from the terrace of the recommended "Bridge Café".

→ **Directions:**
   The village is on the main north–south route which leads through the Soča valley.

→ **GPS:** 46.08538, 13.6343

ALMOST TOO BEAUTIFUL –
Soča, Lepena

The Soča valley and its side valleys are a wild-swimming paradise in themselves. One of the most beautiful and easy-to-reach spots is along the upper reaches of the Soča by the bridge that leads to the Lepena valley. After a gorge-like section, where the Emerald River narrows to a few metres, the valley becomes a little wider. White, bizarrely carved rock formations and deep crystal-clear pools invite you to sunbathe, swim, dive off the cliffs and watch the trout.

Due to the thousands of Instagram posts of the location, as well as its attractiveness and easy accessibility, it may become difficult to find space during the summer months. This applies to both the chargeable car parks on the side of the road and the coveted spots in the sun. As is often the case in Slovenia, during peak season it is advisable to travel here by bicycle to avoid parking issues. Also, choose your timing well, visiting at the beginning or end of the day to ensure undisturbed wild swimming. Another advantage of these less-frequented times of day is that they provide the best light for taking pictures!

→ **Directions:**
Between Bovec and Trenta, take the turning off the main road into the Lepena valley and park right next to the bridge that spans the Soča.

→ **GPS:** 46.3363, 13.64563

A GRANDIOSE SPECTACLE OF NATURE –
Šunikov water park

Close to the best-known Soča bathing spot, the Lepena joins the Emerald River. When hiking or driving upstream along the Lepena, you may wonder whether – given the often low water levels – a visit to the "water park" would make any sense, but karst streams can be deceptive! They often trickle away into the ground (at least in parts) only to reemerge much more powerfully in another location. It is also possible for a calm flow in a wide riverbed to be fed by a wild torrent in the river's narrower, steeper upper reaches.

With regard to the depth and quality of its bathing pools, the river Lepena becomes more interesting from its lower reaches upwards, and the waterfall is its impressive finale. What all pools here have in common is the refreshing water temperature, even in high summer. "Water park" is indeed a suitable name for this grandiose spectacle of nature, best explored on a well-routed hiking trail that always stays close to the stream.

→ **Directions:**
From the main road between Bovec and Trenta, take the turning into the Lepena valley and cross the bridge over the Soča. Then follow the Lepena upstream until you reach the signposted car park.

→ **GPS:** 46.31265, 13.65793

Most na Soči is located at a rocky ridge where the river Idrijca joins the dammed Soča. Archaeological findings prove that people first settled in this region over 3,000 years ago, and more than 7,000 Iron Age burial sites have been detected.

The lake offers ideal conditions for stand-up paddlers, anglers, cyclists and joggers. You can also hire boats and go on organised round trips on the reservoir. Beautiful swimming spots are to be found on the right-hand shore immediately below the road to Sela (a). Here it is easy to park the car and there is a lawn for sunbathing and, within walking distance, a bar selling chilled drinks and snacks. However, even more attractive is the bathing spot immediately at the mouth of the Idrijca (b), below the centre of the small village. You won't find any sunbathing lawn or "beach" bar here, but instead you can swim the Idrijca upstream, circle the remnants of a former jetty and use them as a bathing island. In addition, the village provides parking space and catering facilities.

b)

b)

→ **Directions:**
From the north, follow Route 102 through Tolmin towards Most na Soči. Coming from the south from the Soča valley on Route 103, take a right-hand turning at Sela. If you are coming from the south, from the Idrijca valley, take Route 102, direction Tolmin, until you reach Most na Soči.

→ **GPS:** a) 46.15913, 13.74274
    b) 46.15198, 13.74153

a)

b)

PRETTY AND STILL ACCESSIBLE –
Upper reaches of the Idricja

A short distance downstream of the source of the "young" river Idrijca in a remote karst mountain range near Vosko, there are a few pretty bathing spots that are relatively easy to get to from the nearby road. Although there is generally little traffic on this minor road, these spots are rather suited for brief swimming stops because they are not in full sun and space for lying down is limited.

Beautiful bathing pools (a) are to be found near the idyllic "Wild Lake" where, sadly, swimming is prohibited. At certain times of the year, this karst spring, which delivers up to 60cm3 of water per second, becomes the source of the Jezernica stream. After a mere 55m, this stream joins the river Idrijca, and is therefore regarded as the shortest stream in Slovenia. Another popular and well-kept bathing spot is Naravno kopališče Lajšt (b). This spot is close to the village of Idrijca Bela, where the smaller Belca flows into the river Idrijca.

→ **Directions:**
If you are coming from the north, having passed Most na Soči, follow Route 102 alongside the river Idrijca. Still within the parish boundaries of Idrija, at a wayside chapel, turn right to Gregorčičeva ulica to get to the upper reaches and to Idrijska Bela. Approaching from the south, exit the E61 motorway at Logatec and follow Route 102. When you get to a wayside chapel, turn left to Gregorčičeva ulica to get to the upper reaches and to Idrijska Bela.

→ **GPS:** a) 45.97602, 14.02102, b) 45.96325, 13.98063

a) A distinctive stone bridge of the Wocheiner railway spans this gravel beach on the Idrijca where it joins the river Bača. The latter river also features a few bathing spots but these tend to be no match for the deeper pools and more consistent water levels of the Idrijca. During peak season, the water quality is constantly being monitored in Bača pri Modreju, and it is also during this time of year that mobile snack stalls are on site. A few years ago, a somewhat fragile

diving tower was erected from scaffolding materials on the opposite shore. More recently, floodlights for midsummer beach parties were installed on the bridge pier.

b) At Slap ob Idrijci, it is possible to bathe in pools both upstream and downstream of the weir. These pools are up to 5m deep and, in summer, can reach temperatures of up to 22°C.

→ **Directions:**
From the north, having passed Most na Soči, follow Route 102 alongside the river Idrijca up until bis Bača pri Modreju (parking near the railway bridge) or Slap ob Idrijci. From the south, exit the E61 motorway at Logatec. Then follow Route 102, initially to Slap ob Idrijci and then to Bača pri Modreju.

→ **GPS:** a) 46.14375, 13.7674, b) 46.11947, 13.8037

14

MAGICAL LIKE A FAIRY TALE –
The source of the Soča

According to an ancient fairy tale, once upon a time the gods Triglav, Jalovec and Mangart lived near Trenta. When, one day, an evil water demon appeared and flooded the entire valley and all of its villages, the gods felt the need to intervene. They decided to keep the feared water-spouting demon captive in a cave and only kept his mouth open to the extent that he was able to irrigate the valley without causing further damage.

In fact, the source of the Soča is in the parish of Trenta. Here it surfaces from a dark rock crevice below the mighty peak of the Jalovec. Then it collects in a crystal-clear spring-fed pool, before cascading down into the valley over rocky edges and waterfalls.

A 20-minute uphill hike on a steep path, which is not suitable for children, leads very close to this fascinating spectacle of the natural world. From the upper rock formations you can enjoy a majestic view of the upper Soča valley and the surrounding mountain giants. If you want to take a refreshing bath, you need to be agile, because the source pool itself is an extremely narrow space and the rocks are both sharp-edged and slippery. Down in the lower section, the terrain is more open and easily accessible. Even when sitting in the garden of the inn at the start of the hike you will still be able to watch and listen to the multisensory experience offered by the young river Soča!

→ **Directions:**
From the road between Bovec and the Vršič pass, at serpentine 49, take a left turn and park by the "Soča Spring" inn. Here is the starting point of a steep trail which – in its upper part – is secured with chains, stepladders and steel ropes and is well-signposted. It leads you right up to the spring.

→ **GPS:** 46.41203, 13.72385

15

AT TIMES, "SMALL" CAN BE BEAUTIFUL TOO –

Savica waterfall

Despite its name being in the diminutive form (of "Save"), the Savica waterfall is one of the mightiest and most impressive in the whole of Slovenia. While the name of the "Velika Savica", which forms the waterfall, means literally "Big Small Save", its nearby sister "Mala Savica" has to content herself with the meaning "Small Small Save". Slightly further down in the valley, both streams eventually join. From that point onwards, the by now "Small Save" (the Savica) flows into Lake Bohinj (or Lake Wocheiner). It exits the lake as a river called Wocheiner Save, before finally joining the Wurzener Save at Radovljica. From this point, the river finally carries the non-diminutive name "Save".

The magnificent Savica source waterfall is itself off-limits with respect to bathing. A short distance below the ticket office, where a small fee is charged for the pleasure of using the trail, you can have fun at a very pretty swimming spot underneath a romantic stone bridge. The water that rises from the depths of the Triglav, however, is not recommended for those who prefer a nice hot shower in the morning!

→ **Directions:**
  Exit the E61 motorway at Bled. Follow Route 209 up until the eastern shore of Lake Bohinj and then follow the signs for Ukanc/Slap Savica until you reach the car park. The steep trail is well-secured and its many steps lead you high up into the mountains.

→ **GPS:** 46.28981, 13.79932

THE TWO FACES OF
Lake Bohinj (Bohinjsko jezero)

This enchanting alpine lake at an altitude of 525m above sea level is located in the Triglav National Park. It is 4,100m long, 1,200m wide and up to 45m deep. After heavy rainfall, the lake's water level can quickly rise by 2 to 3m. At the same time, fast-flowing torrents can thunder down the steep hillsides, carrying vast quantities of gravel and boulders into the lake. The Savica also moves a great amount of stones and gravel downstream, forming a constantly growing delta.

While the southern shore of the lake, alongside the road, is quite developed with restaurants, boat hire and sports and adventure tour operators, the northern shore is much more remote and picturesque. It is on the northern shore, in particular, where, in the course of a 3-hour hike round the lake, a good number of romantic bathing spots are waiting to be discovered by wild swimmers. The crystal-clear water of the lake, which is completely renewed by confluence about three times a year, is a paradise not just for swimming and those who like watersports but also the great variety of fish species that thrive here.

→ **Directions:**
Exit the E61 motorway at Bled and follow Route 209 through Bled, alongside the Wocheiner Save, to get to the lake.

→ **GPS:** 46.2816, 13.84745

NOT JUST THE FISHERMAN'S FRIEND –

Wocheiner-Save near Polje

After the Wocheiner-Save has flown through the lake of the same name, it turns into an emerald ribbon while approaching its next "stop", Lake Bled. Before the alpine stream reaches the weir at Soteska, it is rather tame. This means that not only fly fishers but also skilled kayakers and wild swimmers can enjoy the mesmerising water.

A beautiful spot, which is also easy to reach, is between the hamlets of Polje and Kamnje. Here there is a car park, Portaloo, picnic table and entry ladder. At times, you will need to share the pool with the fly fishers, but it is a reasonable size for sharing.

Depending on the water level, you may want to try your wild swimming luck in the Mostnica stream, a small tributary of the Wocheiner Save at Stara Fužina.

→ **Directions:**
Exit the E61 motorway at Bled and follow Route 209 through Bled, alongside the Wocheiner Save, until you get to the small car park in Polje, by the side of the road.

→ **GPS:** 46.2699, 13.91241

ENCHANTING AND FAMILY-FRIENDLY –
Gremčica waterfall

Not very far from the riverbed of the Wocheiner Save is another gem of Slovenia, a country blessed with waterfalls: the Gremčica waterfall. The source of the river Gremčica is to be found on the Jelovica upland plateau. From there, the river makes its steep way down into the Wocheiner valley through a gorge that is also used for canyoning. At the bottom end of this gorge, the stream falls over a 7m drop into an emerald pool. While the terrain by the waterfall has an alpine character and that part of the pool is quite deep, the banks that face away from the fall are flatter, and the water there shallower. This results in a family-friendly gravel beach that is great for lingering or having a picnic. It should be possible to take a robust pushchair, designed for rougher surfaces, up to that point.

The edge of the fall can be reached via a narrow, ascending path. From there, after carefully considering the water level of the pool, you can jump into its depth.

→ **Directions:**
Exit the E61 motorway at Bled and follow Route 209 through Bled, alongside the Wocheiner Save. Park at the railway/bus station in Nomenj. The hike is on an untarmacked track past a car park that is reserved for anglers and canyoners. Cross over a footbridge, then keep to the right. The waterfall is approx. 25 minutes from there.

→ **GPS:** 46.28467, 13.99628

A RIVER BATHING SPOT IN NATURE –

Wocheiner Save Nomenj

The small village of Nomenj is located on the road between Lake Bohinj and Lake Bled in a narrow valley carved by the river Save into the bedrock between the upland plains of Pokljuka and Jelovac. In summer, the meadows and slopes near the river are covered with a carpet of wild orchids that can only be found in this particular region. The footbridge across the Wocheiner Save, now flowing at a leisurely pace and displaying a mesmerising green shimmer, can be reached from the village with a 15-minute walk.

On the left bank, next to the bridge, beautiful bathing spots can be found both upstream and downstream, and some of them even have a small sandy beach. Cross the footbridge and keep to the left. After a few minutes of walking you get to the ruins of the Emas blast furnace, where hydropower was employed to operate furnaces for melting the iron ore once mined here.

→ **Directions:**

Exit the E61 motorway at Bled and follow Route 209 through Bled, alongside the Wocheiner Save. Park at the railway/bus station in Nomenj. The hike is on an untarmacked track past a car park, reserved for anglers and canyoners, to a footbridge. The bathing spot is to both sides of the footbridge.

→ **GPS:** 46.2853, 14.00523

SLOVENIA'S ONE AND ONLY ISLAND –
In Lake Bled (Blejsko jezero)

Slovenia's best-known lake, with an island of the same name, is located on the southern slopes of the Pokljuka upland plateau at an altitude of 475m above sea level. On the island are a church dedicated to St Mary and important archaeological sites dating from the Middle Ages. If you don't swim to the island, there are easier options in the form of traditional wooden boats called "Pletnas".

Lake Bled is approx. 2.1km long, up to 1.4km wide and up to 30m deep. During the summer months, the water can warm to 25°C, and the lake also has an international reputation as a championship rowing venue. Bled castle towers above the northern shore with its public baths – steeped in tradition – and with bathing jetties, as well as 25m swim lanes in the lake. The photograph shows the "wild-bathing spot", which is hugely popular with local people and is located on the opposite, southern shore, near Villa Bled. Apart from offering wonderful views of the lake, island and castle, there is a big sunbathing lawn, Portaloos, SUP board rental and nearby bars and restaurants.

→ **Directions:**
Exit the E61 motorway at Bled and follow Route 209 to the southern shore of Lake Bled.

→ **GPS:** 46.35998, 14.09459

KNOWN GORGE, UNKNOWN RIVER –
Radovna

Meltwater from the Krma and Kot glacier valleys feeds the Radovna stream, whose upper reaches are somewhat hidden between Mežakla and Pokljuka in the Triglav National Park. In spring and early summer, the hummocky meadows in this area are a dazzling display of wild flowers.

a) A little further down the valley is the "chalk lake". Up until 1985, chalk was exploited here in open-pit mining. After mining had been abandoned, the pit filled with water, and today it forms a lake where bathing is permitted, and whose shore is popular in summer. The opaqueness of the water has resulted in a few accidents when people have dived into what was an unknown depth, because obstacles underwater are hard to see from the shore.

In the course of its downhill run, the river Radovna has carved its path between the distinct peaks of the Horn and the Borst. This is the Vintgar gorge, one of Slovenia's most-visited destinations. In this gorge, which is worth visiting and where an entrance fee is charged, you must stay on the secured trails. Hence, and sadly, swimming is impossible here. At low water levels one can swim in the plunge pool downstream of the visitors' section of the gorge – obviously with the utmost caution. This breathtaking 13m river fall, the Slum waterfall, is the highest in Slovenia!

b) Further downstream, before the Radovna joins the Save, and away from the hustle and bustle, is the bathing spot shown in the photograph.

→ **Directions:**
a) Exit the E61 motorway at Lipce and follow Route 634 until Spodnje Gorje. There, turn right to Krnica. From here, follow Route 907 up the Radovna until you can see the "chalk lake" on your right.
b) Exit the E61 motorway at Lipce and join Route 634. Immediately afterwards, turn left to Blejska Dobrava and drive through the village. Then take the footpath to the Sum waterfall and the lower entry to the Vintgar gorge.

→ **GPS:** a) 46.41704, 13.99183
b) 46.40108, 14.10147

JUNGLE CAMP –
Wocheiner-Save
at Radovljica

While the source of the Wocheiner Save is in the Triglav National Park, the source region of the Wurzener Save is in the area around the Karawanks tunnel. From here, flanked by the Karawanks and the Julian Alps, the Wurzener Save flows south-east via Jesenice and joins the Wocheiner Save at Radovljica. The terraces of the romantic old town allow wonderful views of the confluence of the two rivers and the Save water meadows. It is easy to see that bathing is possible here all year round.

As is often the case with bridges, access to the river is much easier here, because in most other locations the riverbanks are densely overgrown with vegetation and almost jungle-like. The spot shown in the photograph is at the Wocheiner-Save, close to the confluence of both rivers, and a big sandbank invites you to sunbathe and watch the water flow by. When the water levels are right, this is a good spot where the Save can be used as a natural counter-current facility for "swimming on the spot".

→ **Directions:**
Exit the E61 motorway at Radovljica and follow the signs to idyllic Kopra. Immediately after the Save bridge, turn right and drive upstream to the next bridge where you can park on the other bank. Further upstream are other bridges with more suitable bathing spots.

→ **GPS:** 46.34236, 14.14152

A GEOLOGICAL FAVOURITE –
Dovžan gorge

Tržiška Bistrica is the name of the wild mountain stream which has cut this very steep gorge into the hard Paleozoic rock of the high-altitude valley. It is the bizarrely shaped rock formations and towers that make the area a favourite with Slovenian rock climbers. Also, there is no other place on earth with such a variety of Permian fossils as the Dovžan gorge, which is why it is a real geological hotspot. And if things get a bit too "hot", you can quickly cool off in the pools of the Bistrica. But be careful: the currents here can be extremely strong and a bathing spot should be selected with great care! Families

with small children will definitively find better, safer options for bathing elsewhere.

Suitable for families is the hiking trail leading from the village of Čadovlje to the distinctive road tunnel that was constructed 100 years ago, opening up the gorge for traffic and transport. At the upper turning point of this trail are a hanging bridge and allegedly the best bathing spot, which is also used by the locals on hot summer days.

→ **Directions:**
   Exit the Ljubljana–Jesenice motorway at Podtabor and drive towards Tržič. Pass the town and continue upstream until you reach the small car park before the tunnel and above the footbridge.

→ **GPS:** 46.38584, 14.33043

OFF THE BEATEN TRACK –
Lomščica waterfall

Getting to this small waterfall requires a certain pioneering spirit! To jump into the wild waters of this fall, an option that is really only applicable in spring and after prolonged periods of rainfall, you need to walk off the beaten track. This means that the trail can be muddy and slippery. In addition, the descent to the fall's plunge pool is covered in raspberry bushes, stinging nettles and areas of slippery rock and boulders.

You can make the ascent easier by not moving straight along the banks of the stream but by first ascending through a meadow near a house. Please be aware that this is private property and be respectful. Those who are willing to face such adversities, and provided that the water level is sufficient, will be rewarded with a memorable and remote wild-swimming experience.

→ **Directions:**
From the mining town of Tržišk, drive alongside the river Bistrica towards Jelendol until you get to an electrical substation on your right. Park here or by the river bank. The arduous 15-minute uphill trail starts on the right-hand bank.

→ **GPS:** 46.37153, 14.32552

REMOTE BUT CHARMING –
Stegovnik waterfall

After having traversed the Dovžan gorge, the high-altitude valley stretches much further than one would think until, finally, first Jelendol and then the tiny hamlet of Medvodje are reached. In autumn 2018, a devastating flood destroyed many properties in the valley as well as severely damaging the road through the gorge, which, for a few weeks, could only be accessed on foot. Jelendol is surrounded by large forests. It is for this reason that, in the early 20th century, the entrepreneur Baron Karel Born built a sawmill, including a small hydropower station, and 5.5km of plant-owned railway tracks. Today, forestry remains one of the main industries of the region.

Accordingly, the starting point for the hike to the Stegnovik waterfall is the car park by a large lumber yard in Medvodje. From here, a moderately steep, signposted hiking trail leads past the "football stadium" and along the banks of the stream to the waterfall. The fall is in a rather shady place on the slopes of the mountain of the same name. It cascades over an approx. 15m-tall rocky step into a mini pool that is just big enough for a dip. During severe winters, when the fall freezes, ice climbers use these ideal conditions at the waterfall in search of an adventure.

→ **Directions:**
  When approaching from Tržič, continue through the Dovžanova soteska gorge up until Jelendol. Then, after a further 3km, park by the remnants of a former military post at the lumber yard in Medvodje. Follow the signposted trail to the right towards the Stegovniški slap waterfall.

→ **GPS:** 46.40224, 14.39754

The source of the Kokra is in the Austrian–Slovenian border region near the Seebergsattel at an altitude of approx. 1,800m above sea level. Having completed its 41km course, the Kokra joins the river Save at Carniola (Krain or Kranjska). In a side valley, the Bistrica, a right-bank tributary of the Kokra, has been dammed, forming a small lake (a). The less frequented Jezero Črnava (Black Lake), which is named after a small dark wood, offers easily accessible and family-friendly bathing options. Also, you can have something to eat on the lakeside terrace of the "Bor Hotel" and enjoy the terrific views of the small lake.

When coming from Carniola (Krain or Kranjska) and driving upstream by the crystal-clear Kokra, the valley narrows upstream of Potoče and soon begins to form interesting ravines that, water levels permitting, attract wildwater kayakers. However, before the valley becomes really narrow, large gravel banks and pools invite you to bathe (b). In Potoče itself is a picnic place where wooden tables and benches have been set up in the immediate vicinity to the river.

→ **Directions:**
   Exit the E61 motorway towards the Seebergsattel border crossing. In the small village of Preddvor, turn left to the Schwarzsee (Black Lake) (a). To get to the bathing spot by the upper reaches of the Kokra (b), continue driving to the Seebergsattel.

→ **GPS:** a) 46.30292, 14.42546, b) 46.30335, 14.47873

a)

b)

b)

IDYLLIC DIP WITH A STEEP ASCENT –
Ank waterfalls

Jezersko is a real Slovenian mountaineering village and one needs certain "mountaineering skills" to earn the pleasure of a dip in the small pool of the lower Ank waterfall. It is not that the trail is suspended or hazardous, but in its middle section it is truly steep. In spring or after prolonged periods of rainfall, the last section of the trail, which leads through forest, can become very slippery.

Together, both Ank falls, which are at an altitude of approx. 1,240m above sea level, have a height of nearly 7m. While the lower fall forms a wide fan-like shape, the water of the upper fall collects in a tight jet.

Just before the climb to the waterfalls starts to become really steep, above the Ank farmstead, you pass the well-known mineral spring of Jezerska Slatina. A word of caution: even if it is tempting to quench your thirst in this spring, please be aware that the healing water, due to its high magnesium content, is known as a laxative!

→ **Directions:**
   Approaching from the Seeberg main road, you can park in one of the public car parks by St Andrej church or in the village centre. Then follow the signposted trail to the waterfalls. Starting at the church, the challenging ascent takes approx. 35 minutes, whereas from the village centre you will need approx. 1 hour.

→ **GPS:** 46.41935, 14.5125

A "HEARTY" PLEASURE –
Lake Planšarsko

Those with an interest in geography may ask what gave the Seebergsattel and the "Seeland" (Jezersko), on the Slovenian side of the border, their names. Is it really possible that a small, heart-shaped lake, the Planšarsko jezero, which was created by the local population by means of damming, was the name giver for such a big region? Certainly not. Rather, the naming of the entire area can be traced back to a mighty glacier lake that, in the ancient past, covered large parts of the valley bottom, and only disappeared as a result of a major earthquake around 1348 AD. Hence, today's lake is merely reminiscent of its considerably bigger predecessor.

In summer, you can explore the extended network of bicycle and hiking trails around the lake; in winter, cross-country ski trails attract winter-sports lovers. The best access points to the lake for swimming are along the north-east shore, while the somewhat more open-spaced sunbathing lawn on the eastern shore is mostly waterlogged. The lakeside restaurant offers not only local specialities but also a magnificent panoramic view of the Kamnik Alps and Karawanks.

→ **Directions:**
   If you are coming from the south, drive through the village of Zgornje Jezersko and follow the road towards the Seebergsattel up until a right-hand turning to the signposted road to the lake.

→ **GPS:** 46.40301, 14.51611

IMPOSING FINALE OF THE LOGAR VALLEY –
Rinka waterfall

In 1987, the Logar valley, which is regarded as one of the most picturesque alpine valleys in Slovenia, was declared a landscape park. This high-altitude valley is 7km long and ends below Kar Okrešelj. Up there, at approx. 1,280m, is the source of the river Savinja. Very soon into its course, this mountain stream cascades 90m in a free-falling spectacle. Depending on the water level, the dip or "shower" in the fall's plunge pool can be more or less intense. However, having crossed only a few rocky ridges below the pool, the water disappears in the sharp-edged scree, only to re-emerge further down the valley.

At summer weekends, in particular, the Logar valley and waterfall are popular excursions with the locals. Therefore, it is recommended to schedule your visit around the beginning and end of the day. It is an unforgettable experience to watch the sunset from the "Eagle's Nest" inn, which seems to stick to the bare rocks. Here you have far-reaching views of the Logar valley and surrounding mountain ranges.

→ **Directions:**
   If you are approaching on Route 428, either from Solčava or the Paulitschsattel, take the turning to the Logar valley and follow the road until you reach the car park by the waterfall.

→ **GPS:** 46.37084, 14.59281

JUST FOLLOW THE DRAGONFLIES –
Repov waterfalls

Right up until World War II, the area of Luče had more than 20 mills. Today, the more than 250-year-old Žagerski mill is the last operating example, although the mill wheel is mostly stationary because the water has been redirected to bypass it. The mill is the starting point of the recommendable nature trail that leads to the waterfall, taking about 25 minutes walking time. The trail passes Petkova mlaka, a biotope that is home to a particularly rare species of dragonfly whose image is depicted on the signposts to the fall. Soon the trail forks to the right and leads through a gorge with several smaller falls.

The actual Repov falls comprise three consecutive rocky steps with a total height of approx. 25m. The pretty pool of the bottom fall can be accessed via a small wooden ladder. After having crossed the stream on a wooden bridge, you can make the ascent to a viewing point from where you have a great overview of the cascades. In winter, this place is full of giant icicles, but watch out for the potentially difficult ascent with steep terrain.

→ **Directions:**
At Stahovica, take the turning to the Črnivec Pass and follow the road through Kranjski Rak and the Volovljek Pass (1,029m), direction Podvolovljek, until you can spot the Žagerski Mill below the road.

→ **GPS:** 46.30789, 14.70805

FOR THE SPORTY –
Savinja

With a length of 92km, the Savinja is the longest Slovenian river that originates in the country. Close to its source, the young and untamed stream cascades down to the Logar high-altitude valley, where it forms the 90m free-falling Rinka waterfall (27). It is because of three tributaries in the form of further wild mountain streams that the Savinja carries sufficient water nearly all year round. As a result, the Savinja, alongside the Soča and Wocheiner-Save, is one of the most "sporty" rivers in Slovenia, and ideally suited for wildwater rafting, kayaking, angling and wild swimming.

In the upper Savinja valley near Radhua (a), suitable swimming spots are few and far between. Also, the strong currents make swimming much more challenging. Further down the valley, the spots are much more family-friendly, for example at Camp Menina (b), where the water temperature can be up to 24°C, and is easy to access.

→ **Directions:**
From Paulitschsattel, initially follow Route 428. Then, from Juvanje, follow Route 225, direction Topovlje. If approaching from the south, exit the E57 motorway at Topovlje onto Route 225. Drive upstream until Juvanje, and then continue on Route 428.

→ **GPS:** a) 46.36084, 14.76012, b) 46.31092, 14.91107

b)

ANGLERS PREFERRED, SWIMMERS TOLERATED –

Lake Smartno

Lake Smartno is one of the biggest man-made lakes in Slovenia and, because of its proximity to Celje, the town's residents are very fond of it as their local recreation area. There are all kinds of activities taking place around the lake, especially hiking, jogging, bicycling and boating, but foremost is angling. It is partly due to the profitable sale of angling licences that anglers are given preference over all other leisure seekers. With its remarkable size of more than 11 hectares. as well as its abundance of fish species and the fact that quite a few record-breaking specimens have been caught here, the lake is a favourite with lovers of angling.

According to the local tourist information board, which we explicitly questioned on this issue, and to many locals we spoke to, swimmers are generally "tolerated". The board explained that the explicit bathing ban, which is clearly stated on information boards by the lakeside, is intended to underline that swimming would be at one's own risk, and that the tourist board won't be held liable for any accidents. For this reason, please be particularly respectful and sensitive at this lake, which is so very abundant in fish but also a haven for long-distance swimming. Hopefully, in this way, we can ensure that swimmers will remain "tolerated" visitors.

→ **Directions:**
Exit the E57 motorway at Celje but do not take the turning southbound towards the town itself. Rather, turn off towards the north and follow the signs to Runtole/Šmartinsko Jezero.

→ **GPS:** 46.31092, 14.91107

A GLAMOROUS FOREST LAKE –
Lake Blaguš

Until very recently, this man-made forest lake was an untouched gem and hardly known, except by anglers. This changed when, in autumn 2019, the "Charming Slovenia – Forest Glamping Resort Blaguš" opened for business. However, in contrast to many other lakes, day visitors are not excluded. Instead, the resort is keen to create a deliberate coexistence of glampers and day-trippers. It is nice to note that (at the current time) the use of the car park and lake is free of charge. Also, a few lovely cycling and hiking trails have been created by the resort operators.

Since the lake is not particularly deep it warms up quickly and offers pleasant bathing temperatures quite early in the season. Please note that bathing is only permitted in specific areas and that certain stretches of the shoreline and lake are reserved for anglers. The dam and several bathing jetties, a small bistro and a pizzeria are located on the eastern shore. The creatively designed glamping accommodation is placed both below the dam and on the northern shore. The quirkiness doesn't end there. The resort also comprises a "forest library" and offers shoemaking workshops.

→ **Directions:**
Approaching from the highway between Maribor and Murska Sobota, take the Sveti Jurij ob Ščavinci exit, then follow the signs to the resort.

→ **GPS:** 46.56768, 16.00174

THE SOUTH
OF SLOVENIA

In this book, "The South of Slovenia" includes all spots to the south of the capital Ljubljana, described from west to east and from north to south.

Roughly in the centre of Slovenia, you find karst phenomena that are typical for the country. The karst rocks harbour mighty karst springs as well as extended cave systems and "disappearing" rivers – streams and rivers that run on the surface for a certain distance but then disappear below ground. There are also what one would call "periodic" lakes. The best-known periodic lake, which is also the biggest in Europe, is Lake Cerknica, with its unique hydrology, fauna and flora.

In summer, the flatter south-east of the country is dominated by the Kolpa, which has pleasant stream-like temperatures and marks the boundary to Croatia over a distance of more than 100km. The Slovenian Riviera is in the south-west of the country. Despite Slovenia's Mediterranean coastline measuring a mere 47km, it features some particularly beautiful beaches, an impressive reminder of the variety that this small but wonderful country has to offer to people who love swimming.

The south of Slovenia

One of the most beautiful beaches along the relatively short Slovenian Riviera is Strunjan Nature Park with Cape Strunjan, Cape Ronek and Cape Kane and their characteristic "Flysch" cliffs. These form fantastic coves that protrude out into the sea and are only accessible via steep trails or by walking along the beachfront. The access to the best-known of these coves, Strunjan moon cove, is so narrow that it is only possible at low tide.

I recommend that you schedule this particular access requirement into your round trip to the moon cove. Please note that parking in the Strunjan Landscape Park is only permitted in signposted, chargeable car parks. Parking by the roadside or wayside is not allowed and is strictly policed! When walking from the big car park in Strunjan, it is up to you whether you hike along the beach first and return via the cliffs or vice versa. Whatever you decide, the sights on the cliffs – Saint

Mary's church and the Strunjan cross – offer breathtaking panoramic views of the cliffs, the coves, the entire Gulf of Trieste and even, given good visibility, Mount Triglav.

→ **Directions:**
Exit the A1 motorway at Koper, then follow Route 111. At the big roundabout ahead of the salines, turn straight to the right and park in the big chargeable car park.
For walking the round trip, please see the above description.

→ **GPS:** 45.53872, 13.61205

In ancient times, the "fat small cape" (the literal translation of Debeli Rtič) was very sparsely populated because, due to the shallow water and many underwater rocks, it was impossible to build suitable harbour facilities here. It was only much more recently that the cape's suitability for wine-growing was recognised. Today, Vinakoper operate one of Slovenia's most productive vineyards in this location. In the long run, however, the land will be gradually eroded, because the sea removes up to 2cm of fragile Flysch rock from this stretch of coastline every year.

The narrow strip of beach, which has formed in front of the cliffs, consists of the remnants of crushed rocks that have been polished into nice round shapes by the ever-moving sea. The water here is very shallow so that the water temperatures along this bit of coarse-gravel coastline around the cape are generally quite warm. It is only in the aftermath of gales, when the waters around this highly exposed cape have been churned up, that the temperatures are lower. After such events, in particular, you should tread with caution along the cliffs because of the increased hazard of falling rocks.

→ **Directions:**
Exit the H5 dual carriageway at Spodnje-Škofije and follow Route 406 towards Ankaran until you reach the "Lazarett Beach" car park on the right-hand side of the road. Park here and hike along the coastline to the cape.

→ **GPS:** 45.59342, 13.70752

Like Rome, city of seven hills, the town of Vipava, which has seven springs, can look back at a turbulent history. In ancient times, the Celts settled in the area, and the name Vipava was derived from the Celtic term "Vip", meaning river. Around 394 AD, one of the bloodiest battles of antiquity between the Western and Eastern Roman Empires, which secured the final victory of Christianity over the old Roman religion, took place in the vicinity of this town.

Vipava's seven springs are located in the foothills of the Nanos karst uplands and flow into the riverbed of the Vipava in the shape of an upturned delta. From there, and before long, the river meanders in a leisurely manner through the famous wine-growing region and picturesque water meadows, where in past centuries a great number of mills operated.

In the bathing spot shown in the photographs, local people set up tables, benches and even sculptures from driftwood, which are worth seeing. This makes the bathing spot not just ideal for river bathing but also for a picnic. It goes without saying that you should take all your rubbish home with you.

→ **Directions:**
From Vipava, take the road to the well-known wine-growing village of Slap and park either by the small Močilnik bridge or the Rouna vineyard. Continue from there on tracks, either by bicycle or on foot, until you get to the bathing spot under a canopy of lush green leaves.

→ **GPS:** 45.85072, 13.94005

Between the high plateaus of Nanos and Trnovo, the river Bela cascades into a gorge, which is also a favourite with rock climbers. Further downstream, near Vipava, the "town of seven springs", the Bela joins the river Vipava. There is a highly recommended gorge hike that starts from the wine-growing village of Vrhpolje and leads past mills, smithies and magnificent pools.

The Vipavska Bela rock-climbing area is regarded as one of the most versatile in the whole of Slovenia. The aptly named Devil's Chair climbing rock alone offers more than 100 climbing routes for all levels of ability.

To allow the climbers to cool down after their challenging ascents, a small "river bath" has been built into the rock face at the bottom of the cliffs. To achieve this, a rocky edge was heightened to make a dam, thereby creating a pretty pool. A small slide and "diving tower" have even been fitted on the banks of the natural swimming pool. But please be careful when using them: they might not necessarily be in the best state of repair and also the water might not always be deep enough!

→ **Directions:**
From Vipava, follow the road to Vrhpolje. From Vrhpolje, either take the signposted gorge trail or continue driving uphill through the village until you reach a small car park by the Devil's Chair. The car park is the starting point for the steep descent to the stream. Parts of the trail are secured.

→ **GPS:** 45.87284, 13.97332

Cave swimming in the Planina

In contrast to Greek mythology, there is no "hell's dog" barking at this entry to the underworld. Instead, the river Unica thunders here, sufficient water levels permitting. The Unica originates from the confluence of the rivers Pivka and Rak, which is another 500m into the cave. This underground confluence is one of the biggest in Europe. You can visit it on a guided tour that lasts several hours, and it can also be navigated by boat. In the near future, I will also operate such tours, during which you can swim in the river's channels as well as in other lakes inside the cave. Just swimming in the massive portal of the 7km-long cave (Slovenia's longest underwater cave) is an extraordinary experience, because in the freezing 8°C water, which is as clear as crystal, it seems as if one is travelling between different worlds. Please be cautious, both when swimming near the edge and also at the very slippery entry into the pool.

→ **Directions:**
   Exit the E61 motorway at Unec and follow the signs to Planina. At the end of the village, follow the signs to "Ravbar Tower" and, a short distance ahead of it, take a right-hand turning. From the small car park, a narrow trail leads uphill through the woods to the cave entrance.

→ **GPS:** 45.82085, 14.24649

Once upon a time, the mediaeval Haasberg chateau was one of the most beautiful stately homes in Slovenia. Today, it is a forlorn place and an impressive ruin. Only a few metres below the castle, an imposing road bridge spans the young river Unica which, coming from the Planina cave, flows towards the Planinsko Polje karst field. The Unica, the "river of seven names", is a moody "disappearing" river that flows alternatingly aboveground and underground. At low water levels it disappears before it even reaches the village of Laze. However, when its confluence exceeds 60m3 per second, the so-called "disappearance holes" are no longer able to divert sufficient amounts of water and, as a result, the 11km2 karst field is flooded.

There is a small car park next to the bridge, on the right-hand bank, by the river. Depending on the water level, this bathing spot can be either extremely family-friendly or a raging torrent. In any case, the proximity to the castle and bridge makes this spot a lovely place for a picnic.

→ **Directions:**
Exit the E61 motorway at Unec, follow the signs to Planina and park by the stone bridge across the river Unica.

→ **GPS:** 45.82872, 14.26404

In the karst region of Lower Carniola, at an altitude of 420–450m, are the caves of Škocjan, which were formed by the river Reka. Around the caves are a great number of sinkholes that were washed out of the porous limestone by rainwater. Over time, some of these sinkholes have been blocked and sealed by organic matter or subsequent input of loam so that rainwater collects in them, eventually forming small, idyllic lakes and pools. Some of the pools even contain small karst springs which, depending on the season and the underground water pressure, can produce copious amounts of fresh water. In most cases, the two types of spring can be distinguished by their colour and water temperature.

One of these nameless pools, which is presumably of the second type, can be found close to the road that leads to the Škocjan caves. I leave it to you to find out whether fairies, water spirits or adventurous local teenagers are the ones who most love the swing that hangs from a tree here. Whatever the case, this swing is great fun, as is swimming in the "fairy pool"!

→ **Directions:**
Exit the E61 motorway at Unec and follow the signs to the Škocjan cave, but don't take the turning to the cave. Instead, continue on the road towards the Hotel Rakov Škocjan until you can see a small car park to your right and the "fairy pool" to your left.

→ **GPS:** 45.79058, 14.29353

Lake Cerknica

In fact, Lake Cerknica can be both! This is because it is a "periodic" body of water, a karst lake, which means that it can either have a size of up to 38km2 or disappear completely. When the lake is full, it is up to 10m deep and is the biggest of its kind. German philosopher Immanuel Kant was fascinated by this phenomenon, which he described in 1756 as follows: "It has a few holes in its bottom, but it doesn't drain through those before around St Jacob's Day, as this is when it suddenly disappears, including all of the fish. Then, after having left the ground to dry and turning it into good pasture and fields for a period of three months, around the month of November, it reappears as suddenly as it left." With this kind of lake, you can never be completely sure whether it will actually be there when you visit and be at all suitable for swimming. But there is one thing along the shores of Lake Cerknica that you can count on. Throughout the year, and irrespective of the status of the lake, you will find unique flora and fauna. Even in the most severe winters, when the lake freezes and turns into a gigantic natural skating rink, the lake remains enchanting and beautiful.

→ **Directions:**
   Exit the E61 motorway at Unec and initially follow the signs to Cerknica and then to Dolenje Jezero, where you can park.

→ **GPS:** 45.769, 14.35539

Despite being named after Slovenia's capital, this remarkable river carries that name for only about 41km of its entire 85km journey through Slovenia. Otherwise, the Ljubljanica travels different lengths of its course under the names of Stržen, Cerkniščica, Unica, Logaščica, Pivka and Rak.

Along the river section that includes this particular bathing spot, artefacts from different eras of human history have been discovered. This suggests that the river was once regarded as sacred and that these artefacts were offerings to the river deities.

Noticeboards by the road bridge at Brezovica point out that collecting and removing ancient finds is prohibited. One must say that the darkish water and dense covering of aquatic plants would make any sighting rather difficult. In summer, there is a good chance of getting chilled drinks and snacks from the small bistro on the left bank, approx. 200m downstream of the bridge, where paddlers can tie their boats.

→ **Directions:**
Exit the E61 motorway at Brezovica and follow Route 742 towards Podpeč until you reach the bridge across the Ljubljanica.

→ **GPS:** 45.974730, 14.419350

From the pilgrimage church of St Anne, situated high up on a hill of the same name, you have wonderful views across the Ljubljana Marshes and the small lake, which is almost a circle and is sometimes called "Krimsko". This lake is fed by seven karst springs underneath the nearby wood and it runs off into an underground funnel more than 50m deep. Despite its depth, the small lake pleasantly warms up for swimming. As a result, it can get rather busy along the shoreline, especially at summer weekends.

You may find that the free car park on the edge of the wood is as full as the small sunbathing lawn in front of the lakeside restaurant. There is also a bathing jetty with an entry ladder under old limes. This is much frequented by the village youths who dare each other with acrobatic dives, whereas the youngest bathers tend to paddle at the shallow shore area. The lake is also in great demand as an all-year-round anglers' paradise since it rarely freezes completely in winter and boasts a good stock of giant silver carp.

→ **Directions:**
Exit the E61 motorway at Brezovica and follow Route 742 to Podpeč. From there, follow the signs to Jezero.

→ **GPS:** 45.969360, 14.432290

Krka at Žužemberk

Two mighty karst springs in the vicinity of the village of Gradiček feed the Krka, the only river in Slovenia where limestone tuff forms sediments. This sedimentation occurs when dissolved lime accumulates on aquatic plants in shallow water. Subsequently, after the plants have died, porous sediments form. The Krka features around 90 such limestone terraces, one example being in the ancient village of Žužemberk, below the castle hill. Throughout the centuries, these terraces were chosen as perfect locations for mills.

Slightly further downstream is the green town beach of Žužemberk, called Loka. It is easier to access than the natural pools on the limestone terraces, as well as being shallower. In summer, generous free parking and sunbathing lawns under the wide canopies of large ancient trees, as well as fun treehouses, sports and playing areas, and the popular Loco Loka Bar, bring numerous visitors to this attractive spot. From here, you have a great view of the old town with its characteristic castle, in whose courtyards mediaeval festivals and tournaments are held. You can rent boats and eat well in the Koren Guesthouse by the green beach.

→ **Directions:**
Exit the A2 motorway at Trebnje and follow Route 650 to the Krka valley.

→ **GPS:** 45.82805, 14.93053

Kočevje mining lake

Around the 14th century, German-speaking colonists from Carinthia and Tirol settled in this densely wooded area and began clearing the land. The settlement was raided by the Ottomans and burnt to the ground on several occasions. In 1893, the town was connected to the railway system, thereby opening it up for open-pit mining of brown coal. During World War II, the dense forests offered a hideout for partisans, and today they are the habitat of the brown bear.

Apart from the textile and chemical industries, forestry remains the most important economic sector to this day. When open-pit mining was abandoned, because it had become unprofitable, the pits gradually filled with water and are now used as local recreation areas. Lake Kočevje is very close to the town. The shore that is next to the town has a big car park, a small snack stall and a few wooden platforms and bathing jetties. There are, of course, other access points to the lake, but they are often occupied by anglers.

→ **Directions:**
From Ljubljana, follow Route 106 to the former mining town. In the town, follow the signs and park immediately by the lake.

→ **GPS:** 45.64567, 14.8717

For anyone living in the Alps, karst springs are a fascinating sight. While springs in other parts of Europe are mostly tiny trickles of surfacing water, in karst regions they are frequently large, watery blue eyes that produce such copious amounts of water that, only a few metres from the source pool, they have turned into substantial streams with a serious current. The source of the river Krupa, which is located below a 30m rock face near the village of the same name, displays this phenomenon. The young river joins the Lahinja after a short journey of only 2.5km. Today, it is hard to imagine that only 40 years ago this idyllic spot was seen as one of the most polluted rivers in Europe. At that time, incorrectly stored industrial waste resulted in extreme levels of polychlorinated biphenyls (PCB).

Proof of the restored water quality is the existence of an endemic olm subspecies as well as a cave mussel that had been thought to be extinct. The spring, which owes its intense turquoise colour to special minerals, has been protected as a conservation site since 1997. In recent years, a round-trip nature trail has been created. It begins immediately at the spring-fed pool and leads past three watermills and across a hanging bridge to a Stone Age cave, before returning to its starting point. If the undergrowth is too dense to access the source pool, it is possible to swim in the stream below the weir, against the current. However, the water is freezing, and so this suggestion is intended for hardy types!

→ **Directions:**
 Exit the A2 motorway at Novo mesto and follow Route 105 up until Jugore pri Metliki. From here, follow Route 421 to Semič, then take a left-hand turn to the village of Krupa.

→ **GPS:** 45.6349, 15.21675

The Kolpa at Podzemlj

The Kolpa is a superb river for all kinds of water sports, but visitors are often confused by its different names, all of which are very similar. The Kolpa (in Slovenian), Kupa (in Croatian) or Kulpa (in German) has its source in the Risnjak National Park in Croatia. Over a distance of roughly 100km, it marks the border between Slovenia and Croatia. The river is much loved by anglers and recreational kayakers for its pleasant summer temperatures and because it is seen as a clean body of water, at least up until Karlovac in Croatia. It therefore also attracts large numbers of bathers. During the summer months, a multitude of events take place on the river, such as the Schengenfest rock festival at the Vinica campsite or the summer carnival in Podzemelj. The village of Podzemelj is on the river's left bank and, like most Slovenian Kolpa villages, is part of the Bela Krajina region, which means "White March", a name derived from the countless birches native to this part of the country. Just outside the village, by the river, is a popular campsite that is open to day-trippers who want to bathe here (for a small car park charge). The site features bathing jetties, sun-bathing lawns, boat hire and a nice restaurant.

→ **Directions:**
Exit the A2 motorway at Nove Mesto and follow Route 105 to Metlika. Continue on Route 218 through Podzemlj until you reach the car park by the campsite.

→ **GPS:** 45.60453, 15.27708

Roman ruins around the village of Otok, which belongs to the parish of Metlika, show that this region was settled as early as antiquity. Towards the end of World War II, partisans constructed a basic airfield close to the village, which was used by the allied forces. Today, a Douglas C-47 transport plane serves as a memorial to the supply and medical evacuation missions that were flown from Otok airstrip. If you are lucky, you may be able to spot wild birds in the water meadows by the Kolpa around the village: grey herons, storks and ducks, in particular.

The Kolpa has a wide drainage basin with a size of 10,032km², mostly on Croatian soil, and a mean drainage volume of 283m³ per second at the point where it joins the river Save. However, while wide, the river is along many stretches not deep enough for swimming. To utilise the Kolpa's hydropower, people have from ancient times built dams and weirs along its course. To this day, these weirs that belong to sawmills and watermills provide beautiful pools that are both easily accessible and perfectly suited for bathing and swimming. The pool at Otok is a great example.

→ **Directions:**
 Exit the A2 motorway at Nove Mesto and follow Route 105 to Metlika. Continue on Route 218 until you get to the turning to Potok.

→ **GPS:** 45.61289, 15.29701

There were once about 90 mills on the banks of the river Kolpa, whereas today only one is in continuous operation, at Kočevje on the Slovenian side of the border. This mill was built by the ethnic German minority of the Gootscheer. However, on the Croatian bank, many of these mills have now been restored (in Pravutina, Mala and Jurovo, for example). An old proverb from the region says, "Water that has already flowed past cannot power a mill." Therefore, people created dams and redirected the water into narrow channels so that its energy could be used to power mills of all kinds.

The hugely popular and extensive bathing spot by the dam at Griblje owes its existence to this type of ancient construction work, which also benefits a sawmill on the Croatian side that is still in use today. Age-old trees provide ample shade and the big sunbathing lawn features a few fire pits.

→ **Directions:**
Exit the A2 motorway at Nove Mesto and follow Route 105 to Metlika. Continue on Route 218 downstream until you get to Griblje. Then follow the signs to the mill.

→ **GPS:** 45.56978, 15.29774

A prominent bend of the river Kolpa reveals a ford which was formerly of great strategic importance. Hence, local rulers constructed the mighty Freyenthurm Castle, now in ruins. Under the legendary Field Marshal Johann Freiherr von Lenkowitsch, it was once a key fortress that protected the region from the Turks. It served its purpose well because the Turks never managed to seize it. However, Freyenthurm was severely damaged in World War II and used by the local population as a store for building materials during the post-war reconstruction of their burnt villages.

The path to the river Kolpa is quite steep as it leads downhill under a shadowy canopy of leafy branches. In a few places, one can actually see the old castle ruins. Having reached the river level, the path initially passes a simple campsite. Then, after a sharp bend to the left, Domačija Kuzma is reached.

The well-preserved buildings include both a sawmill and a working watermill that can be visited for a fee on a guided tour. Further down the farmstead and dam is a family-friendly gravel beach where the water is quite shallow. However, better suited for swimming is the area above the dam itself, and access is made easier by means of a small wooden jetty. There is even a tiny bar that serves homemade wine and schnapps, as well as other chilled drinks and a selection of snacks.

→ **Directions:**
A2 junction Nove Mesto, take Route 105, until Metlika. Then on the 218 downstream, direction Adlešiči, until you reach the signposted turning to Domačija Kuzma.

→ **GPS:** 45.53133, 15.31362

The romantic idyll by the banks of the Kolpa is somewhat disturbed at Adlešiči. As a result of the refugee crisis, from 2015 onwards, the border on the Slovenian side was first "secured" with barbed wire and later with a tall wire fence. Since it was the dams, in particular, that were used by many of the refugees to cross the river Kolpa, these areas are still marred by wire fences. Thankfully, more recently, local campaigners and tourist operators in the region have brought this issue to the attention of the public. They demand that these "protective installations", which have now become obsolete, are taken down, especially because the fences don't just impair tourism but also prevent the free movement of game and other wild animals.

Despite these issues, the restored Trzok weir offers one of the prettiest wild-bathing spots, with a summer water temperature of up to 28°C. It is suitable for families as well as non-swimmers. The bank area is called the "old land", and here the Jankovic campsite provides camping and glamping facilities in small wooden bungalows from May to September. During the summer months, you can sit out on a covered terrace by the river and enjoy roast lamb or a pig roast, accompanied by the region's great wine.

→ **Directions:**
   Exit the A2 motorway at Nove Mesto and follow Route 105 to Metlika. Continue on Route 218 downstream, towards Adlešiči. Then follow the signs to Kamp Jankovič.

→ **GPS:** 45.52092, 15.3227

THE SOČA

THE LIFE CYCLE OF AN
ICE-COLD BEAUTY

Adventurous and ravishingly beautiful. This is how the Soča presents itself from its fairytale-like source at the foot of Mount Travnik to its mouth by the Gulf of Trieste, south of Monfalcone. Depending on the sunlight and the river's immediate environment, its crystal-clear ice-cold water shimmers in either sky-blue or emerald hues. It is no surprise that the Soča attracts not only the rare Marmorata trout but also those who like water sports.

The Soča is called Isonzo in Italy and in Roman times carried the rather apt name of Frigidus. From its very beginning, the river is very lively. Immediately after it leaves its source pool near the Vrsic Pass in the Triglav National Park, the Soča enters a steep cascade towards the village of Trenta. Then it forces its way through narrow gorges up to 15m deep, where it is spanned by several precariously swinging hanging bridges. In the village of Soča, it is joined by the Lepena tributary from the left, and at Bovec the river Koritnica flows into the Soča from the right.

Between the joining of the Lepena and the exit from the big gorge at Kobarid, the Soča's varied and in parts challenging wildwaters bring out the best in kayakers and rafters alike. At Most na Soči, the wild river is tamed for the first time – that is, dammed. Subsequently, it flows past Tolmin and through the picturesque village of Kanal ob Soči in a southerly direction. Due to the valley's opening towards the south and the Mediterranean Sea, this alpine valley has a mild climate, favouring agriculture and fruit production.

From Gorizia, the river brushes past the northern Italian lowlands, where it finally becomes the Italian Isonzo, transporting, as a torrent, vast quantities of gravel and debris into the Adriatic Sea. Over time, frequent flooding in the Isonzo's delta has created a wetland that is the habitat of rare plants and animals and that is reminiscent of the Camargue in Provence.

IN ANOTHER ERA – *IN ANOTHER COUNTRY*

Peace didn't always prevail in this valley, which appears so very idyllic today. More than 100 years ago, the bloodiest battles of World War I were fought in the Soča valley. In a total of twelve Battles of the Isonzo, hundreds of thousands of soldiers were killed, a tragedy documented by Ernest Hemingway in his novel *In Another Country*.

Today, the war cemeteries, monuments and museum in Kobarid, along with the 230km Walk of Peace, are all reminders of this terrible time, a time when people didn't have the leisure to enjoy the natural wonders of the beautiful Soča valley. All of us who are able to do this today, in peace, should feel truly blessed.

CROATIA

MUCH MORE THAN JUST HOLIDAY COASTLINES, BEACHES AND ISLANDS

The Republic of Croatia emerged from the multi-ethnic state of Yugoslavia by declaring its independence in 1991. It was able to defend this newly founded independence during the Croatian War, which lasted until 1995. The country, which is called "Hrvatska" in Croatian (abbreviated to HR), borders Slovenia in the north-west, Hungary in the north, Serbia in the north-east, Bosnia and Herzegovina in the east and Montenegro in the south-east. As an exclave, the most southerly part of the country, the former Republic of Ragusa around the major city of Dubrovnik, doesn't have a direct land connection to the rest of Croatia's territory. The two territories are divided by Bosnia and Herzegovina's access to the Adriatic Sea. This is a strip of land only a few kilometres wide, soon to be "bridged" by a monumental construction project.

In many ways, Croatia is deemed to be a country in transition. It is quite telling in respect of both the geographical and the socio-demographic development of Croatia that the country has provided the locations for German-produced Westerns as well as several episodes of the fantasy series Game of Thrones. The former were made in "Red Indian Territory" (that is, in the remote karst regions of continental Croatia), whereas the latter were filmed on the characteristic beaches (and in the picturesque towns) of South Dalmatia. Descriptions of Croatia's beaches, coastlines and islands alone would fill many volumes, and there is ample literature available on that subject matter already. Therefore, while this book does feature those sites, it predominantly focuses on providing information about the lesser-known and rarely mentioned wild-dipping and wild-swimming spots in the

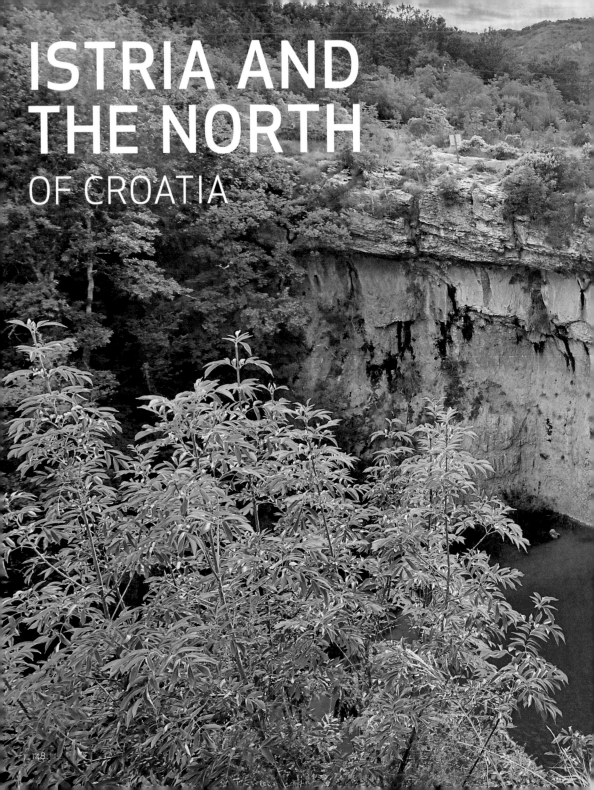

ISTRIA AND THE NORTH
OF CROATIA

This section of the book includes all spots on the Istria peninsula, continental northern Croatia and the northern Adriatic Sea down to Crikvenica. The spots are described from west to east and from north to south.

The coastline of the western Croatian region of Istria is approx. 540km long. Parts of this coast are divided by fjord-like inlets, such as the Limski Channel with its well-known mussel beds. The majority of the beaches are either rocky or gravel beaches, so that sandy beaches are more of an exception. The inner part of Istria is sparsely populated, and many villages are situated in picturesque locations on hilltops, from where there are wonderful views right up to the coast. Since the peninsula is mostly made up of limestone rock and the cooler seasons can bring great amounts of rainfall, the conditions are ideal for spectacular waterfalls. The southernmost tip of Istria has been turned into the extensive nature reserve and wild swimming paradise of Cape Kamenjak.

Continental northern Croatia comprises the lowlands alongside the rivers Save and Kupa, the mountainous region of Zagore north of Zagreb, the Medimurje between the rivers Drau and Mur, the mountains of Gorski Kotar between Rijeka and Karlovac, and coastal sections of the northern Adriatic Sea. These regions offer incredible opportunities for swimmers: from cave, spring, river and coastal swimming

Istria and the north of Croatia

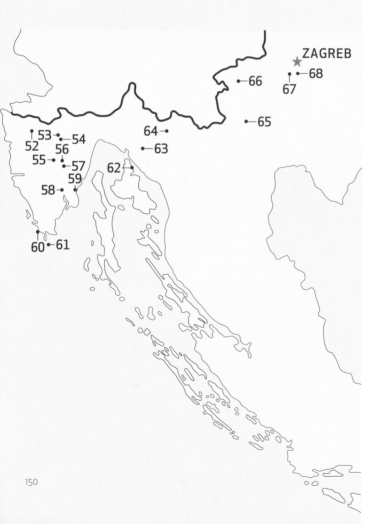

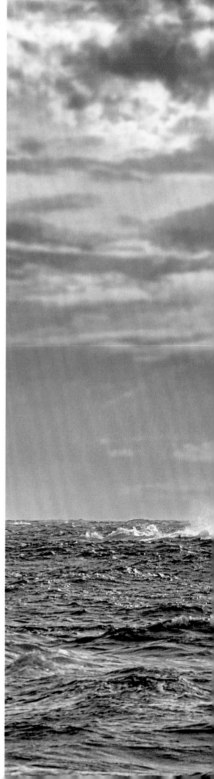

A SPOT FOR NATURE LOVERS AND POETS –
Butori waterfall

Among the many karst phenomena that you can admire in Croatia, the Butori waterfall is one of the dreamiest. Above the fall, the Jugov potok stream meanders in a leisurely manner until it meets a rocky barrier, and then abruptly cascades into the depths! Below the approx. 10m fall, a lake has formed in a mossy cauldron. It is guarded by tall trees and the water in the cauldron drains away into the ground there and then, only to re-emerge somewhere else, further downstream.

Local youths have attached a rope to one of the trees that you can use to swing like Tarzan out into the middle of the small pool. A note of caution: the rope is very slippery, and you should also attempt to land in the middle of the pool as, if it is there at all during the hot summer months, it is not particularly deep. In August of each year, nature poets from all over Europe congregate in the small clearing above the Butori gorge to give atmospheric lectures in the light of torches and campfires.

→ **Directions:**
Approaching from Buje, continue in the direction of Oprtalj. Then, having driven through the village of Marušići, follow the signs to the waterfall.

→ **GPS:** 45.41356, 13.77376

WOULD YOU LIKE ANYTHING ELSE, SIR/MADAM? –
Buzet waterfall trail

Given sufficient time and stamina, it is possible to visit seven waterfalls on a single trip, beginning at Buzet. Starting at the local waterworks, the trail leads via Selca, Glistonja and Kuhar to Kotli, before returning to where the car is parked. Those who feel that the 14km round trip, which takes approx. 5 hours to complete, is not enough, can add a detour to Hum, the "smallest town in the world". If you don't just want to hike along the Mirna and admire this river, but also want to bathe in waterfalls, the best times of the year are spring and autumn, or in the summer after prolonged rainfall.

On the hike, which mostly follows the course of the river, you can admire not just cascades and bizarrely washed-out stretches of rock but also a great variety of orchids and butterfly species – as well as daredevil rock climbers. It takes about 2.5 hours to get to Kotli mill (see 54), a recommendable stop on your hike. Along the way, you pass four waterfalls with pretty pools that are suitable for bathing, water levels permitting.

→ **Directions:**
   Take Route 44 to Buzet and then turn off towards Juričići. Park by the waterworks and follow the signs to Staza sedam slapova.

→ **GPS:** 45.39344, 13.9924

Hum –
the smallest town in the world

In days gone by, the village of Kotli was known for its tailors and especially its millers, and in its heyday had 100 inhabitants. When the village was electrified, the mill on the river Mirna, which was frequently damaged by flooding, was abandoned, and so the village residents were forced to leave their traditional stone houses because their source of income had gone. Today, the "cauldron village" (Kotli = cauldron) can also be reached by car. Here, waterfall hikers coming upstream from Buzet get to the river's fifth cascade and find an ideal resting place in the form of a nice *gostilna* (inn).

Apart from the romantic "mill waterfall", there are two further waterfalls to admire and swim in above Kotli. Also, you shouldn't miss out on a visit to the picturesque "ghost village" itself. The same applies to the inn, which offers a magnificent view of the mill cauldron. Be careful when descending the slippery path to the pool below the mill to swim.

Gjork waterfall

Zelenscak waterfall

→ **Directions:**
  From Route 44, at Roč take the turning to
  Hum and, in the village of Brnobići,
  follow the signs to Kotli.

→ **GPS:** 45.36872, 14.01673

GIGANTIC BATHING AND CLIMBING –
Zarečki Krov waterfall

It is hard to believe that there is such a giant fresh-water pool in the middle of Istria, and one that is so easy to get to. Here, the river Pazinčica, coming from Cerovlje, cascades over a 7m rocky ridge whose underside is padded with a softer type of stone. Over time, the river has eroded this rock so that a cave has been created, the ceiling of which offers some of the most difficult climbing routes in Croatia.

From the left bank, a trail leads down to the cave and pool. If you find that this spot is overcrowded, especially at weekends in early summer, you can try your luck further upstream where there are some beautiful, albeit far less spectacular, bathing spots.

→ **Directions:**
Coming from Pazin, join the dual carriageway, direction north-east. Immediately after the railway flyover, at the village sign, turn left onto an untarmacked track and park after approx. 200m.

→ **GPS:** 45.24905, 13.96134

The Pazinčica upstream of the fall

AN OASIS OF COMFORT AND EASE –
Gologorički waterfall

It is hardly possible for a waterfall to be more family-friendly! Apart from the amusing name, this place is so easy to reach and there are also pets for the children to cuddle and a very welcoming agrotourism farm. Given all of the above, does it really matter that the fall pool itself doesn't measure up to Olympic dimensions and is rather shallow? It is more than sufficient for cooling off on hot summer days and small children, in particular, won't ask for anything else.

The actual area of the 3m-high fall is fenced off. This is because of the many donkeys, horses, cows, sheep and rabbits on the farm. But you can enter the fall's enclosure if you wish. Don't miss out on the Agroturizam Dol inn which serves delicious local specialities, has very friendly and attentive staff and is a brilliant source of information about the area.

→ **Directions:**
Exit the E751 at Cerovlje and follow the road until you get to the hamlet of Gologoriča. Park by the Agrotourismo, walk the approx. 200m distance back to the stream, through a small wooden gate, and descend to the water.

→ **GPS:** 45.2462, 14.03591

HIGHLY RECOMMENDED –
Sopot waterfall

Arguably Istria's most stunning and (with a 25m free-falling height) tallest waterfall is in the village of Floricici near Potpićan. Although being in the middle of the peninsula, the unexpected rock formations in this spot suddenly make one feel as if one is on a coastal cliff. On closer inspection, a great variety of fossilised mussels, snails and other marine species can be detected in the limestone. Once upon a time, this location was covered by a primordial ocean.

If you think that the view from above is extremely impressive, wait until you have crossed the centuries-old stone bridge and descended the somewhat hazardous path down to the plunge pool, where breathtaking scenery awaits! Given sufficient water levels, usually in spring or autumn, a vast blue and green basin stretches out in front of you and invites you to take an unforgettable plunge. Another charming option is the Walk of Saint Simon, a trail that begins on the edge of the village of Gračišće and leads right to the waterfall. Along the way, one passes abandoned ancient stone houses, which are hidden away in the forest and overgrown with vegetation, as well as clearings where wild orchids thrive.

→ **Directions:**
From Route 64 between Pićan and Potpićan, turn off to the north, direction Škopljak, and follow the signs to Floricici/Slap Sopot.

→ **GPS:** 45.21888, 14.04405

STRAIGHT INTO THE EYE –
The Blue Eye by the Raša

The Raša is a wild river that is formed by several tributaries, beginning at the hamlet of Potpićan. In antiquity, the river was known by the name of Arsia. It flows southbound through a deeply cut valley. Eventually, it joins the Ria Raški zaljev, which is a former valley, now flooded by the sea. In its upper reaches, the Raša carries little water. In its middle reaches, access is difficult. And the lower reaches have been rectified into a canal-like shape, which means that swimming, while being possible, is not an attractive proposition.

However, if you park in Most-Raša (by the Raša bridge) and walk or cycle approx. 4km upstream, you get to an almost round, nameless karst spring with an iridescent blue hue, given the right lighting conditions. Please be aware that, should you decide to swim in the mesmerisingly fresh and vitalising water, a rope is strongly recommended. The reason is that, because of the tall and extremely muddy banks, it is almost impossible to exit the water without the help of one.

→ **Directions:**
Follow Route 66 to the hamlet of Most Raša between Barban and Labin. Park by the bridge and walk upstream on the right bank, following a gravel track.

→ **GPS:** 45.08251, 14.02957

FRESHWATER POOLS WITH A SEA VIEW –
Sentonina staza

The vibrant coastal village of Rabac and the mediaeval hilltop town of Labin are connected by a modern panoramic road. Another option of going between both places is a hiking trail which is named after the goddess Sentonina and leads past springs, rushing streams and waterfalls. Depending on your stamina and ambition, this trail can be walked uphill or downhill, each leg taking approx. 1.5 hours in each direction. You can take the bus or a taxi to return to your starting point.

If you only want to visit the big waterfall, it is best to park near the big Autocamp by the football ground in Rabac. From here, the trail is on almost level paths and leads through open woodland to the pool of the lowest fall. Further up, one can also bathe in smaller pools, which are significantly more difficult to get to. In return for the challenging ascent, you get peace and quiet and are rewarded with stunning views towards the coast and sea.

→ **Directions:**
   Follow Route 66 to Labin and then continue to Rabac. Take a right-hand turn to Camping Oliva and park there.

→ **GPS:** 45.08393, 14.14269

FULL OF LIFE –
Saccorgiarna cove

Pula has several beautiful bays, coves and sandy beaches. This west-facing beach has the advantage that it is usually still possible to bathe here, even if the Bora winds are churning the sea elsewhere. Also, the cove provides several options for where to put down your towel: sandy beach, gravel beach, rocky coastline, meadow, concrete slabs or the pier.

Adventurous local youngsters, in particular, love this cove. For chilling out in the evening and dancing the night away, people go to the trendy "Zeppelin" bar, which takes its name from an airship that was not just tied down in this particular location during World War I but also shot down in this very spot. The cove is renowned for its breathtaking sunsets!

→ **Directions:**
Approaching from the town centre of Pula, follow the road to the aquarium. When you get to a small wood, take a right-hand turning to the Zeppelin Beach Bar.

→ **GPS:** 44.84235, 13.83466

Ahead of you the open sea, below you aweso-me cliffs for cliff-diving, behind you a peninsula with unique flora and fauna. The southernmost tip of Istria has a great deal to offer. In earlier centuries, this stretch of land, which is now a protected nature reserve, was intensely far-med. But many of the farmers left the region, and as a result the former agricultural area was in danger of becoming overgrown by scrubland. Also, many of the native orchid species were threatened with extinction. For these reasons, pastoral farming is now being supported once again.

Hikers, joggers and cyclists can find terrific trails in the gently undulating terrain, while surfers and kitesurfers love the perfect winds. The 30km-long coastline around the cape has a multitude of marvellous coves for bathing on rock or gravel beaches, while the beaches on the east coast (b) are less frequented and better protected from the wind than those directly at the southern tip (a), the latter being suitable for cliff-diving.

a)

→ **Directions:**
   Keep heading south when travelling through Istria and you can't miss the fishing village of Premantura. Use either the signposted car park in the village or drive straight to the cape – a chargeable option for cars during the peak season.

→ **GPS:** a) 44.76658, 13.92409
   b) 44.78526, 13.91765

b)

a)

b)

b)

A GRAVELLY ADVENTURE –
Havišće beach

Jadranovo is one of the quieter villages on the otherwise lively Riviera of Crikvenica. This particular white-gravel beach is approx. 2km to the south-east of the village centre. Its shoreline is shallow and the rocky cape, turquoise water and lush vegetation all add to the superb scenery. Havišće is ideally suited for families with small children. The beach itself is about 2.2km from the centre of the village. During the peak season, you can hire deckchairs and buy drinks and snacks from a small beach bar.

The coves of Havišće and nearby Lokvišće provide a fabulous view of the barren coastal landscape of the island of Krk. If you prefer to lie down on rocky slabs, you can find these by the southern entry to the cove or hike to the "northern cape", or around it to the very pretty rocky beach at Lokvišće (visible in the background of the drone shot).

→ **Directions:**
Turn off the coastal road to Havišće and drive through the village centre. Follow the signs to Jadranovo-Plaza and park above the beach promenade. Then, in the cove, keep to the right.

→ **GPS:** 45.21965, 14.61692

Lokvišće cove

SWIMMING UNDER BIRCHES –
Lake Lepenica

Fužine is the village with the highest annual rainfall in Croatia. To manage and use these large quantities of rain, which at times exceed 4000L/m2, three reservoirs were built in the region of Fužinarski Kraj. The oldest reservoir, which is Lake Bajer by Fužine, is used predominantly for angling, surfing and boating. People prefer the youngest and smallest Lake Potkos for a picnic, whereas the birch-lined Lake Lepenica is much loved by bathers in summer. When, after a period of heavy rain, the lake is close to overflowing, you can swim a "birch slalom" between the flooded trees!

During the construction of the Bajer reservoir, engineers discovered a small cave that was named "Spilja vrelo" and made accessible to the public. The cave conceals a magical small lake, which has been used as a location for the German-produced "Winnetou" Westerns. I am planning to offer guided tours that would include a legal swim in the lake.

→ **Directions:**
Coming on the E65 motorway from Rijeka, take the Vrata exit. In Fužine take a right-hand turn and follow the road along the shore of Lake Bajer. Pass the Vrelo cave until you can see the sign to Jezero Lepenica on the left. Follow the road until you get to the barrier.

→ **GPS:** 45.32225, 14.70133

SPRING EXPLORATION FOR OLMS –
"CAVE SWIMMING" AT
Zeleni Vir

The upland plateaus of Gorski Kotar ("mountainous land" in English) are dominated by the so-called "green karst". Green karst develops when a thin layer of humus accumulates on the limestone substrate. This humus layer is capable of absorbing the ample moisture, thereby allowing lush vegetation to grow. Below Skrad, in a valley basin up to 300m deep, is the "Devil's Gorge", which was cut into the rocks by the Jasle stream and whose entrance can be reached via a narrow and steep serpentine road. If you don't want to go to hell, but merely to the cave, we recommend an approximately half-hour hike from Skrad's slightly run-down railway station. Depending on its flow and on the light, this spring appears either crystal-clear, emerald green or muddy brown. Only the rear part of the basin is suitable for swimming, where you have sufficient distance from an ugly weir or drainage system of the power station that is located downstream at the entrance to the Devil's Gorge.

→ **Directions:**
Exit the E65 motorway at Ravna and take a right-hand turn onto Route 3, direction Skrad. Before you get to the village, turn off to the left towards the railway station and park there. The trail starts behind the station buildings and enters a steep descent. Once you have reached the valley bottom, keep to the left and follow the course of the stream upstream until, to your left, the free-falling Curak waterfall and, next to it, the mighty cave portal appear. The Zeleni Vir spring is inside the cave.

→ **GPS:** 45.423, 14.89624

65

BATHING FUN IN THE CITY OF FOUR RIVERS –
Korana city beach

Karlovac, the city of four rivers, is traversed by the rivers Kupa, Mrežnica, Dobra and Korana. Because of the excellent water quality, people like to bathe in these rivers, with the river Korana, which drains from the Plitvic lakes, being the preferred location.

The crystal-clear water of this small river has been regarded as having healing properties from prehistoric times, and bathing in the Korona has been popular since time immemorial.

Foginovo, the public city beach in the centre of Karlovac, is the only officially registered river beach in Croatia. In warm summers, the Korana at Karlovac can reach bathing temperatures of up to 28°C. The park-like environment along the river banks includes many sunbathing lawns, sports grounds and restaurants. It is said that, during balmy summer nights, if you are very quiet on the river banks with their ancient trees, you can even listen to the seductive song of the Korana nymphs!

→ **Directions:**
Exit the E65 motorway at Karlovac-Centar and follow prilaz Večeslava Holjevca road. At the crossroads with Ulica 13. Srpnja, turn left and park ahead of the Korana bridge.

→ **GPS:** 45.4843, 15.55933

SOMEWHERE IN NO MAN'S LAND –
Brisalo waterfall

The Zumberak Nature Park close to Zagreb is characterised by the absence of large settlements, hotels and motorways. Instead, you get as much untouched nature as you like, as well as secluded prehistoric sites. It is mainly visitors from the capital who come here on day trips to recharge their batteries and enjoy the great outdoors. The area is known among gourmets mainly for the delicious trout, which are caught in the clear mountain streams, and the black truffles to be found in the extensive "primordial forests".

The "valley of the small waterfalls" (Slapnica) is about 10km long. The Slapnica stream runs through it and it enjoys special protection and care as a nature reserve. While the name-giving stream and other small waterfalls in the vicinity are not well suited for swimming, the Brisalo fall, a beautiful waterfall in a dreamy side valley, is ideal for this purpose (well, at least for a dip). In connection with a mountain-bike tour through the flat but idyllic Slapnica valley, the Brisalo is a destination worth visiting, for families as well.

→ **Directions:**
Follow the E65 motorway or Route 1 to Draganić. Continue in a northerly direction to Krašić and then to Medven Draga. There, take the turning to the Slapnica valley.

→ **GPS:** 45.73693, 15.49126

CITY LAKE FOR OUTDOOR-SPORTS LOVERS –
Lake Jarun

To the south-west of Zagreb is the city's borough of Jarun, close to the river Save and home to the 235-hectare Jarun leisure and sports park, as well as a lake of the same name. The lake, which is divided by several islands and a 2km regatta course, has a sizeable surface area of 75 hectares. The so-called "small lake" comprises both a training and a competition arena where rowing and canoe world championships have been staged.

With regard to bathing and extensive swimming, the "big lake" is much more suitable. A multitude of different bathing spots, including on the islands, give you a choice between "hustle and bustle", sporty, off the beaten track and nudist. A one-way ring road circumnavigates the lake and you can use it with your car for a fee. Bicyclists and pedestrians, on the other hand, have free access.

→ **Directions:**
All roads that lead to Zagreb city centre are signposted for the Jarun borough, which is approx. 7km from the city centre. Once you have arrived in the borough you cannot miss the way to the sports park.

→ **GPS:** 45.78007, 15.91974

URBAN SWIMMING AND EVENT VENUE –
Lake Bundek

This huge park project was created in 2005 as an urban recreational area along the river Save between Liberty Bridge and the Bridge of Youth. Similar to Lake Jarun, there is also a "big" and a "small" lake, with the small one being a treasured biotope and protected nature reserve. This means that bathing is only permitted in the big lake, whose bottom and shores were constructed using countless tons of gravel and whose water quality is constantly being monitored.

There are showers and sanitary facilities all around the lake. In summer, the lakeside stage becomes a venue for events and concerts for up to 2,500 visitors. Right next to the stage, there is safe wheelchair access to the water. Numerous sports grounds, playgrounds and barbecue areas, as well as sanitary facilities and restaurants with lounges, cater for all family requirements and ensure that, even in the big city, hot summer days can be more than just bearable.

→ **Directions:**
Coming from the entry point to the city at Slavonska Avenija, continue to the crossroads at Avenija Veceślava Holjevca, then drive in the direction of the river Save. It is best to park by the Liberty Bridge across the Save, at the racecourse, and walk to the park along the river bank.

→ **GPS:** 45.78487, 15.98758

This section includes all spots between Crikvenica and Šibenik. The spots are described from west to east and from north to south..

Up to Zadar, the almost 150km-long Velebit mountain range dominates this region. The "big thing" (the literal translation) is between 10 and 30km wide and densely wooded on its landward side, whereas the vegetation is sparse on the seaward side. Cave explorers and climbers love this coastal mountain range because of its geology. Sailors, on the other hand, have cursed it at times since it is here that the feared katabatic Bora winds originate. The coastal road winds itself between the steep mountainsides on the one side and the craggy cliffs, which drop down to the sea, on the other. This road offers marvellous views of the offshore islands and there are countless minor roads and untarmacked tracks leading downhill towards idyllic coves.

Despite somewhat disputed definitions, it is generally accepted that the historical and geographic region of Dalmatia begins roughly at Zadar. The Dalmatian landscape is predominantly a rugged karst region that includes the offshore islands as well as the mountainous hinterland. The coastal region from Zadar to Šibenik is particularly fertile.

From a swimmers perspective, the islands and coastline of the region, as well as the karst rivers of the Dinaric mountain range and Dalmatian Zagora, and also the gigantic Lake Vrana, have a lot to offer.

CENTRAL
CROATIA

Central Croatia

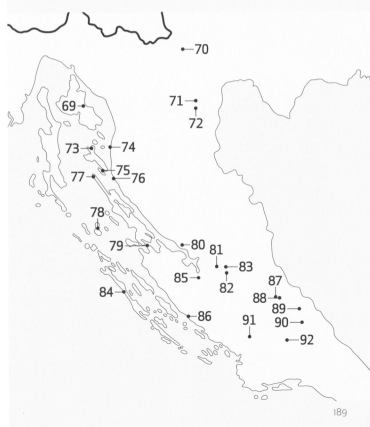

Cres and Krk are the biggest islands in the Adriatic Sea, and Krk is also the one with the most species of amphibians, although the fewest mammals. Very rarely, a brown bear, in an attempt to extend its territory, manages to cross the Velebit Channel that separates the island from the mainland. Human beings are not faced with such problems because we can use the road bridge that has connected the island since its construction in 1980.

With a 200km coastline, Krk boasts many wonderful beaches, of which Javna is one that is more off the beaten track. Vela Javna ("Big Javna") and the adjacent cove of Mala Javna ("Small Javna"), where dogs are permitted, are on the eastern shore of the island by the Velebit Channel. This channel is feared by sailors as a challenging wind funnel and it is recommended that you check the weather for Bora wind alerts before travelling to this spot. To protect your feet from sea urchins and sharp-edged rocks, it is a good idea to wear swim shoes. Also, take sufficient drinks and supplies, because neither of the two coves has any facilities.

→ **Directions:**
   Vela Javna is accessible via the narrow road that connects Vrbnik and Risika on the eastern shoreline and that is merely an untarmacked track in parts.

→ **GPS:** 45.09571, 14.66227

Mrežnica

For almost its entire 64km-long course, the Mrežnica flows over porous limestone. For that reason, this river, in conjunction with moss, travertine and algae, on which the dissolved limestone sediments, has over time formed a multitude of small waterfalls, pools and rocky chutes. Up until today, a total of 93 waterfalls have been counted along the Mrežnica, six of which are taller than 6m. At many of those falls, mills were operated in centuries past. Of those, around 30 remain today, mostly used by the tourist industry either as restaurants or weekend homes. At Belavići, the longest remaining wooden bridge in Croatia is still being used for road traffic.

The excellent water quality and lovely landscape make this karst river a big favourite with anglers, kayakers and rafters. Just be aware that, along some of the more remote sections in the upper reaches, landmines were laid during the Yugoslav Wars. It is therefore best to talk to the locals and make sure that bathing is safe. Sadly, the source of the Mrežnica is located within a restricted military area. Apart from that disappointing fact, this incredibly pretty stream offers magnificent, safe pools that are guaranteed to make every wild swimmer's heart sing.

→ **Directions:**
   Approaching from either Tounj or Karlovac, drive to Belavići and then turn right across the bridge, direction Bukovlje. Park by the side of the main road and follow one of the cart tracks to the river. There are other, beautiful and easily accessible bathing spots below the bridge as well.

→ **GPS:** 45.4124, 15.4802

Like its tributary, the river Mrežnica, the lovely Korana is a typical representative of a karst river. The landscape-forming influence of these rivers finds its most impressive manifestation at the Plitvice Lakes. At the end and outlet of this chain of lakes, more precisely at the Sastavci (confluence) point, where the Plitvica flows into the lakes, is the "official" beginning of the river Korana. In the Kordun region, the river marks the border to Bosnia and Herzegovina for a few kilometres. Apart from the UNESCO natural World Heritage site of the Plitvice Lakes, the best-known river section is in Slujn at the Rastoke natural phenomenon.

Slightly above this gorge and immediately next to the road bridge is an easy-to-reach river bathing spot with car-parking spaces, sunbathing lawn, a small diving tower and stone steps leading down to the water. Here, the Korana becomes deep relatively quickly, but a few hundred metres upstream it is also suitable for children. On the opposite bank is the popular Korana River Bar with a pretty pub garden right next to the waterfalls.

→ **Directions:**
   Route 1 from Karlovac to the Plitvice Lakes leads through Rastoke. Take the turning on the right-hand bank immediately by the road bridge and park the car.

→ **GPS:** 45.12138, 15.58979

The Jesenica stream has its source in the Mala Kapela mountain range but only 6km downstream it disappears into the ground. Subsequently, it flows underground through porous limestone over a distance of more than 20km, before resurfacing approx. 7km south of Slunj, "disguised" as a karst spring. The stream, which shimmers in emerald green hues and which local people also call Slušnica, joins the Korona in a cacophony of noise at Rastoke.

Due to its long journey underground, the water is cold and enriched with calcium. The latter is the reason for the gradual accumulation, over thousands of years, of a 500m-wide and 200m-long travertine barrier ahead of the mouth of the river. The Slušnica cascades into the Korona over this barrier in a total of 23 waterfalls and a total height of 20m. Depending on the flow, the best places for swimming are the source pool of the "supposed" karst spring and the area below the derelict mill. You can also try out the sections further downstream. There can be no question that this natural gem is "out of this world".

→ **Directions:**
Travelling on Route 1 from Karlovac to the Plitvice Lakes, approx. 4km from Rastoke, take the turning to the hamlet of Slunjčica and park by the noticeboards above the spring. The descending hiking trail to the mill and spring takes approx. 10 minutes.

→ **GPS:** 45.07913, 15.58863

Lopar peninsula

In the past, Lopar, to the north of the island of Rab, was a sleepy fishing village, but according to legend it was also the birthplace of the legendary stonemason Marin, founder of the Republic of San Marino. As early as the 19th century, the village became a popular seaside resort due to its fabulous beaches. It also became an early hotspot for nudists, who were particularly attracted by Sahara beach, which has remained extremely popular to this day.

Almost all of the more remote coves, such as Ciganka (a) and Podšilo (b), are to the north of Lopar. They have kept their very natural appearance, are without facilities or infrastructure, and accessing them mostly requires a short walk. However, your efforts will be rewarded with beaches with very fine sand in the central sections of the coves, followed by beautiful rocky beaches along the edges.

Depending on the wind and weather you have lots of choice between various coves. The water quality is excellent throughout and sandy beaches with shallow shorelines, rather a rarity in Croatia, are a paradise for families – once you have got there! Please note that you will have to provide both the shade and the catering!

→ **Directions:**
a) In Lopar, take a right-hand turn just ahead of the ferry port and follow Route 105, direction north, as far as possible. Park by the noticeboards and take any of the beaten tracks to the cove.
b) At the first roundabout in Lopar, take a turn halfway to the right onto Route 105. Always keep to the right and follow the road, direction north-east. Park by the noticeboards and take any of the beaten tracks to the cove.

→ **GPS:** a) 44.84993, 14.72523, b) 44.84593, 14.74672

b)

When following the steep road downhill to the village, which consists of a mere 50 houses, and looking out to the sea, you may wonder why people have put up such a high "diving platform". The answer is unexpected: the so-called "Tunere" from the Malta peninsula were not built for adrenaline junkies but served as lookouts for schools of tuna!

The gravel beach of Lukovo, by the cemetery, is far less frequented than most other beaches on the Riviera of Senj. Here, you can listen to the chirping of the crickets, the air is filled with the aromatic scent of macchia and the sea is crystal-clear. If you are looking for a change of scenery and prefer rocky terrain you can hike to the peninsula or to one of the neighbouring rocky beaches. Small loggias, made of dry stone walls, offer protection from too much wind or sun. Have a rest and enjoy the breathtaking views of the Bay of Kvarn and offshore islands.

→ **Directions:**
Turn off the coastal road to Lukovo and park by the church. Take the steps downhill, past a small restaurant, to the gravel beach in the cove, or hike to the rocky beach on the peninsula.

→ **GPS:** 44.85428, 14.88905

This place is so beautiful that one could easily spend a long chunk of one's holidays in this spot alone. However, this easily accessible beach of fine gravel is equally perfect if you have a little time left until your ferry departs, or if you want to jump into the water immediately after your arrival on the island of Rab. After all, the ferry port is just a few minutes down the road by car, which makes this cove, and neighbouring ones, a very attractive proposition.

Pudarica beach itself, which is not very big, has a small beach restaurant, changing rooms, a shower and a jetty for boats. Due to the shallow shoreline, fine gravel or sand, and the absence of sea urchins, access to the beach is ideal, even for small children. Late-night revellers will love the Santos beach club and its terraces, opening its doors at sunset.

→ **Directions:**
From Route 105, between Barbat and the ferry dock, at the Pudarica and Beach Club Santos signs, turn into the short road towards the beach and park for free by the roadside.

→ **GPS:** 44.70762, 14.83168

In the Zavratnica "fjord"

Almost fjord-like, the Zavratnica cove, which is only a short distance from the ferry port from where you cross to the island of Rab, cuts deep into the karst edges of the Velebit coastal mountains. As a geomorphological natural phenomenon, the cove is a protected reserve. It can be reached via a hiking trail that crosses the centre of the National Park and is chargeable during the summer months. However, the trail passes several pretty coves along the way, to which you can descend and where you can always find a quiet spot when the main cove of Zavratnica is overcrowded.

In high summer, it is best to visit the central section of the cove – which is approx. 1km long and between 50 and 150m wide, and for which an entrance fee is charged – at the beginning and end of the day. At those times you can swim undisturbed in the clear water to the wreck of a Siebel ferry (a shallow-draft catamaran landing craft operated by the Germans during World War II). It was sunk by British fighter bombers in this location during the war and now rests on the seafloor at a depth of only a few metres.

→ **Directions:**
Turn off the coastal road and initially follow the signs to the ferry for the island of Rab, and then take a left turn to Jablanac. When you have reached the start of the hiking trail, park by the side of the road.

→ **GPS:** 44.70024, 14.90337

Tovarnele

The village of Lun at the most northerly point of the island of Pag – known for its cheese – also has a worldwide reputation for its olive groves. Of the 80,000 olive trees in this area, around 15,000 are wild. These are up to 8m tall and 1,500 years old! There are only three such locations in the world, which is why the wild olive grove has been declared a protected botanical reserve and can be explored on a nature trail.

Lun itself is not by the sea. To hear the gentle lapping of the waves you need to go to the fishing village of Tovarnele, which is about 1km down the road. A short distance outside the village are magnificent gravel and rocky beaches, which may be without facilities but instead reward you with fantastic views of the surrounding islands of Dolfin, Cres and Lošinj.

→ **Directions:**
Approaching from Novalja by car, Lun is reached on the main road. Otherwise, travel from Rab to Lun by passenger ferry.

→ **GPS:** 44.69278, 14.73627

a)

b)

Spared from mass tourism, the Dalmatian island of Olib is located in the azure-blue sea, approx. 50km north of Zadar and east of its neighbouring island of Silba. The island was once densely populated but today only about 150 people permanently live on and in Olib, the only village on the island. Traditionally, the islanders made a subsistence from agriculture and fishing. More recently, small-scale sailing and day-tripping tourism have been added to their source of income. The island's landmark is a 400-year-old watchtower that was built to protect the community against pirates and that is part of the island's coat of arms.

Thanks to the absence of cars, big hotels and noisy nightclubs, Olib is a true refuge for nature lovers in need of rest and recuperation. Dreamy coves, some of which can only be reached by boat or on foot, hold the promise of unforgettable bathing experiences. The island's largest bay, "Olib Bay", is on its west coast. Slatinica (a), the cove with the most beautiful sandy beach, is on the eastern shore and thereby more exposed to the winds. Well protected from the Bora wind, on the other hand, is Sveti Nikola cove (b), with its small church dedicated to Saint Nikola.

→ Directions:
You can travel all year round with the passenger ferry from Zadar. Once on the island, walking is the way to get about.

→ **GPS:** a) 44.3853, 14.79353
b) 44.35539, 14.77365

It was during one of the conflicts with the Ottomans in the 16th century that, according to local lore, the shepherdess Jelena Grubišić had a vision of the Virgin Mary on this small island, and was instructed by the saint to build her a church. As soon as this had been accomplished, the statue of St Mary, which the Turks had looted, miraculously returned to nearby Nin, one of the oldest Christian communities in Croatia. In memory of this event, a pilgrimage from Nin to the tiny island of Zečevo takes place three times a year.

This swimming spot is not just fascinating because of its history but also because of the Velebit mountain range that provides a stunning backdrop. Despite there being not much of a beach as such, you can use the narrow pier and the jetty to put down your towels. The spectacular sunsets, for which the region around Zadar is widely known, are even better from this very special spot. Apart from a few fishermen, leisure boats and flocks of sheep, there are very few other visitors to the island. You are pretty much on your own here and able to fully immerse yourself in the untouched, barren beauty of the place.

→ **Directions:**
The road to the island leads straight through the town of Vrsi, which is close to Nin. Pass the church on your right and then follow a rough track for the last kilometre until you reach a narrow ford that separates the island from the mainland. It is best to cover the remaining 800m on foot.

→ **GPS:** 44.29548, 15.19349

WINNETOU
5

a)

The Paklenica National Park, 30km north-east of the city of Zadar, has gained a reputation far beyond the borders of Croatia as a climbing paradise, with more than 400 routes at every level of difficulty. In Croatian, Paklenica means "small hell". It presumably refers to the "rocky hell" that has been created here by the forces of erosion over millions of years.

This wild karst landscape with its distinctive rock formations is so compelling that it was used in 1962 as the location for a screen adaptation of *The Treasure of Silver Lake*, a Wild West novel by German author Karl May. Both in the lower part of the canyon (a) and much higher up near the forester's lodge (b) – now a *gostilna* (inn) – you can enjoy wonderfully refreshing plunges in fabulous pools. Please be aware that, off the beaten tracks, of which there are a remarkable 150km, this rugged region is the habitat of poisonous horned vipers and common adders. Also, and much more ominous, you need to be cautious concerning as of yet uncleared landmines from the Yugoslav Wars.

b)

→ **Directions:**
Travelling on the coastal road, at Starigrad, follow the signs to Paklenica National Park. Park at the end of the road and make your ascent alongside the Paklenica stream.

→ **GPS:** a) 44.31575, 15.48068
b) 44.34543, 15.4829

Waterfall swimming below Barberov Buk

In general, it is fair to assume that any route where whitewater kayakers can have fun, and which isn't overly extreme, will be suitable for wild swimming. This applies in particular to the river Zrmanja, which winds its way through the karst landscape towards the Adriatic Sea over a length of almost 70km and through a total of six gorges.

It is best to explore the multitude of potential swimming spots from a rafting boat or kayak or on extensive canyon hikes. However, for those who haven't got the necessary amount of time, but still want to have fun with magical waterfall swimming, a visit to the easy-to-reach Berberov Buk fall is recommended. Below the wide cascade is a large pool that borders on a lovely sunbathing lawn. Immediately next to the waterfall is a *gostilna* (inn) with a shady pub garden by the waterside.

→ **Directions:**
Turn off the coastal road or the motorway and follow the road to the Maslenica bridge on Route 54, passing through Jasenice, until you reach Zaton Obrovački. Take a left turn onto Route 27 to Muškovci and follow the road through the village to the car park by the waterfall.

→ **GPS:** 44.1979, 15.76691

In the movies, the river Zrmanja became the Rio Pecos and, together with the Zrmanja plateau, provided an ideal location for sections from the German-produced Westerns *Winnetou 1*, *Winnetou 3*, *Old Surehand and Winnetou* and *Old Shatterhand in the Valley of Death*. Those who want to experience this "Native American country" from the water, with an added adrenaline boost, can join organised rafting and kayaking tours from Kastel Zegarski. Tours last 3 to 4 hours, end in Muškovci and provide opportunities for river bathing. During a tour, you will be able to swim, for example, by Visoki Buk, the highest waterfall of the Zrmanja. Rafts

and kayaks need to be carried around the fall anyway, so why not enjoy the water and go wild swimming! Otherwise, this waterfall, close to the mouth of the river Krupa, or the even nearer Ogarov Buk fall can be reached via a hike from the "base camp". This starting point for the rafting tours is by an old mill where you can find beautiful bathing spots upstream and downstream. In summer, you can get snacks and chilled drinks on-site for building up your energy levels before starting on your next adventure in this breathtaking region of central Croatia.

→ **Directions:**
Turn off the coastal road or the motorway and follow the road to the Maslenica bridge, on Route 54, passing through Jasenice, until you reach the turning to Obrovac. Then continue to Kaštel Žegarski and the river and the Riva Rafting Centar "base camp".

→ **GPS:** 44.16043, 15.8541

Although the 17km-long Krupa is a short river it features 19 waterfalls and a pristine river landscape that is arguably one of the most exciting in Europe. Talking of love: according to legend, we owe one of the most beautiful bridges in Croatia to this very emotion. Allegedly, the listed monument of Kudin Most was constructed by Kude, a young man who built the bridge in order to cross the river to join his true love.

There are magnificent swimming spots in the vicinity of the bridge that can be reached by an approx. 40-minute walk (a).

A few kilometres upstream, the road that leads to the village of Krupa crosses the river by Croatia's oldest orthodox monastery. Above the monastery garden, where snacks and drinks are offered during the summer months, you can find easy access to the river for bathing (b).

In the hamlet of Krupa, ahead of the old mill and near the road, is a small picnic area and bathing spot (c).

→ **Directions:**

Turn off the coastal road or the motorway and follow the road to the Maslenica bridge, on Route 54, passing through Jasenice, until you reach Zaton Obrovački. Take a left turn onto Route 27, passing Muškovci, direction Krupa. Then turn right to the Kudin Most car park (a). From the Kudin Most turning, continue in the direction of Krupa until you get to the Krupa bridge by the monastery (b). Follow the road to the hamlet of Krupa and park ahead of the mill (c).

→ **GPS:** a) 44.1883, 15.84575
　　　 b) 44.19049, 15.88739
　　　 c) 44.19246, 15.90936

Sakarun beach

Brbinjščica cove

Dragon's Eye

Dugi Otok

True to its name, the "Long Island" (the meaning of "Dugi Otok") has a considerable length of approx. 45km. It is between 1 and 4km wide and known for its two salt lakes. There is only one road on the island, which stretches through extensive olive groves and from which, at irregular intervals, cart tracks lead to the many beaches. Almost as legendary as the beach at the Golden Horn of Brač is Sakarun beach on Dugi Otok, with its Caribbean feel. The increasing number of day-trippers, who during the summer months come across on the car ferry from Zadar in search of a sandy beach, means that the Golden Horn is rather overcrowded.

The atmosphere on the west coast in the small cove at Brbinjšćica, which offers a choice between sandy and rocky beaches, is much quieter. Here, wild swimmers find two further incredible attractions: firstly, an extremely photogenic rock pool that borders the sea and has the alluring name of "Dragon's Eye", and secondly, to the right along the cliffs, the picturesque sea cave of Golubinka.

Those who get a chance to explore Dugi Otok from the waterside can find superb remote coves in the Telasica National Park, as well as a former submarine bunker that you can swim in.

→ **Directions:**
Take the car ferry from Zadar (in the new port, outside the old town) to Brbinj on Dugi Otok. Between Brbinj and Savar a narrow road leads down to Brbinjšćica beach. From the car park, walk on the road towards the coast and then take a beaten track through the *macchia* down to the sea.

→ **GPS:** 44.05441, 14.98786

Golubinka sea cave

In ancient times, lush beech woods covered the area that gave the region of Bukovica its name ("Bukva" = beech). Today, a karst area with sparse vegetation stretches between Obrovac, Benkovac and Knin. The area is drained by the river Karišnica, which carries water predominantly in spring and autumn. Despite the source of this river being in a small cave behind one of six derelict watermills at an altitude of only 120m above sea level, the Karišnica has formed a multitude of pools and waterfalls over its 2.4km course.

There is a particularly enchanting swimming spot with crystal-clear water near a Franciscan monastery close to the river's mouth and before the new pedestrian bridge. An information board is located slightly uphill by a car park on the bend of the road. Here begins the hike to the Natura 2000 area of the Karišnica valley.

→ **Directions:**
Exit the E65 motorway at Posedarje and follow the landlocked bay of Novigradsko more until you get to the crossroads after Prigrada. Take a left turn, direction Obrovac, and immediately afterwards another left turn, direction Karin Plaza. Park by the monastery.

→ **GPS:** 44.12818, 15.61952

Lake Vrana

Lake Vrana is an important bird and biodiversity area. In fact, the almost 60km2 nature reserve is an ornithologist's paradise. Croatia's biggest permanent lake almost touches the sea at some points and you can get an impressive overview of the area from the viewpoint on mount Kamanjak. When a canal to the sea was constructed in 1770, the water table decreased by 3m and, as a result, the extensive swamp to the north was drained. Since then the area has been used for animal grazing. Outside the restricted areas, Lake Vrana is a rewarding place for anglers and boaters.

Best for swimming is the camp at Pakostane where, for a small fee, you can park the car and use the existing facilities, including bathing jetties, showers, a restaurant and boat hire. This area was a location for *The Treasure of Silver Lake*, a screen adaptation of German author Karl May's Wild West novel of the same name. A few props remain as reminders of that event.

→ **Directions:**
Exit the E65 motorway at Benkovac and follow the road towards Pakoštane until you get to the camp by the roadside.

→ **GPS:** 43.93301, 15.51348

Skrandinski Buk

I was asking myself this question when, in autumn 2020, I heard from a reliable source that "swimming in the Krka inside the boundaries of the national park was prohibited with immediate effect". Whatever the situation, the 22m-tall Krčić waterfall and the Krka spring directly below are worth seeing. Swimming in the plunge pool doesn't just depend on the responsible authority's permission, but also, and very decidedly so, on the water levels. The statement that "the national park begins downstream of Knin and reaches up to Skradin" leaves room for interpretation of the prohibition.

It is, however, beyond dispute that the Krka is one of the most beautiful rivers in Europe. It is 72km long and carries pure, fresh water over the first 50km to its highest waterfall, Skradinski Buk. In its lower, flatter reaches, on the other hand, until it meets the sea, the water has quite a high salt content.

Until autumn 2020, swimming had been permitted in marked areas, including Skrandinski Buk, and ample use was made of that authorisation by wild-swimming lovers.

→ **Directions:**
Exit the E65 motorway at Pirovac and follow Route 59 via Knin to Kovačić. Then follow the signs to the waterfall.

→ **GPS:** 44.04175, 16.23525

b)

a)

Whenever the water table at the Krčić fall (87) is too high for swimming, it is worthwhile checking out the stream's upper reaches. To get there, follow an untarmacked road past the Krka spring to the hamlet of Kijevo, which gained an infamous reputation due to brutal ethnic cleansing during the Balkan War.

The high valley of the Kričić stream leads one into the impassable wilderness of the Dinara mountain range, which includes Croatia's highest peak. Following the stream, you will find small waterfalls as well as a few pools (a) and several derelict mills (b). The mills are mostly situated by the stream's cascades, downstream of which pools have formed, and these are frequently the best swimming spots. Usually, though, you have an opportunity to try your luck in the main current and the outflowing leat. Especially rewarding is a visit to the Kričić valley in the autumn when the leaves display a tremendous array of colour and the stream is more likely to carry sufficient water.

→ **Directions:**
Exit the E65 motorway at Pirovac and follow Route 59 via Knin to Kovačić. When you have reached the crossroads where a right-hand turn leads to the waterfall, don't take that turning but instead continue straight ahead on an untarmacked track, direction Kijevo.

→ **GPS:** a) 44.03905, 16.26532
b) 44.02722, 16.31694

The foothills of the Dinara mountain range are the location of one of the most fascinating springs in Europe. Glavaševo Vrelo, the most spectacular of the eight sources of the Cetina, is close to the village of the same name. The enormous depth of the spring becomes apparent from the air when the water is still and crystal clear. Up until now, the spring has been explored to a depth of 115m, but its true depth is estimated to be between 130 and 180m.

The water that flows from this mighty source pool is a very cold 10°C. Having left the pool, it runs past the picturesque chapel on the small hill next to it. Not far away are the remnants of the Church of Holy Salvation, the oldest Croatian church dedicated to the Holy Redeemer and a hugely important monument of European sacral architecture. Equally worth a visit is the charming hamlet of Cetina, with its ancient stone houses.

→ **Directions:**
Exit the E65 motorway at Dugopolje and follow Route 1, direction north. Take the turning to Civljane and follow the road until you reach the spring. Park by the small church.

→ **GPS:** 43.97687, 16.42996

235

Only a few kilometres from its source, the river Cetina joins this reservoir which, depending on its water table, can have a size of between 10 and 20km2. During the Yugoslav Wars, Serbian troops allegedly attempted to blow up the reservoir's 70m-tall and 470m-wide dam, which is constructed from aggregate material. The dam was originally built to generate electricity, provide drinking water and protect the area against flooding. It also served as a location for the German-produced Western *The Oil Prince* (1965) and a training facility for the Croatian Rowing Association.

Tourists became aware of the lake's attractiveness when the British broadsheet *The Guardian* voted it third in a competition of European lakes most worth visiting. When the Cetina doesn't have a high water table, its water is pretty clean and ideally suited for all kinds of water sport, wild swimming included. Downstream of the mouth of the Cetina is a campsite, and on a peninsula, around the "Beach Bar", you can find popular bathing spots.

→ **Directions:**
Exit the E65 motorway at Dugopolje and follow Route 1, direction north. Just before you get to Vrlika, take the turning towards Garjak. Pass the campsite, which is on your left, and follow the track to the small peninsula.

→ **GPS:** 43.90076, 16.45203

Not far from the point where the Cikola joins the Krka is this almost circular karst lake with a 150m diameter and 30m depth, which is also a spring. You can enjoy a first glimpse of this natural phenomenon from a viewing point near the village of Goriš. The lake's location in the deeply cut and often flooded fertile valley, with a backdrop of an almost horizontal karst upland plateau, is just breathtaking. Also stunning is the colour of the lake that, depending on the light, displays widely varying tones. Due to the poor state of the tracks that lead downhill to the lake, it is best to leave the car behind and walk to the shore. Even skilled mountain bikers might find the very rough access tracks a real challenge. The only access point to the lake, where the otherwise dense reeds are penetrable, is close to a derelict building where a few fishing boats are moored.

→ **Directions:**
Exit the E65 motorway at Šibenik and follow Route 1, direction Drniš. A short distance after Radonič you get to a left-hand turning to Goriš. From here, drive to the viewing point in the Krka valley. Park the car and take the signposted hiking trail.

→ **GPS:** 43.81707, 16.01399

At the beginning of the Croatian War, the frontline between Krajina Serbs and Croats was right here. The heroism of the Čavoglave battalion, a unit made up of volunteers from the village of the same name, was immortalised in a notorious war song that made the village known throughout the country.

While the karst spring carries little water in summer, often drying up entirely, come autumn and after prolonged rainfall the whole of the spring area can become flooded. From here, the Čikola flows through a fertile high valley to Drniš. Downstream of the town, it forms a deep gorge and, soon after that, joins the river Krka. Swimming is only possible in the northernmost part of the spring. This is the actual source pool, which is somewhat separate from the rest of

→ **Directions:**
  Exit the E65 motorway to join Route 33 to Drniš. Then take a right turn onto Route 56 to Čavoglave. Turn left to Mirlović Polje. This road leads straight past the source lake. You can park behind a B&B and take a beaten track to descend to the source pool.

→ **GPS:** 43.79752, 16.32482

THE SOUTH
OF CROATIA

This section includes all spots south of Šibenik. The spots are described from west to east and from north to south.

The area around Šibenik has gained a worldwide reputation due to the Krka National Park with its spectacular water-falls. Sadly, swimming in this wonderful river, which flows into the Adriatic Sea at Šibenik, has recently become prohibited. Nevertheless, its extensive catchment area in the Dalmatian Zagora, with its unique karst phenomena, is a paradise for wild swimmers. The Dalmatian hinterland includes the region around the towns of Kaštela, Trogir and Šibenik, as well as, in a broader sense, the area of Drniš, Knin, Sinj and Imotski. The Zagora is separated from the sea by the Mosor and Biokovo moun-tain ranges. The former stretches over a length of 25km between Split and the mouth of the Cetina at Omiš. The Biokovo mountains to the south tower above the Makarska Riviera, an area highly develo-ped by the tourism industry, and extends to the fertile delta of the river Neretva at Ploče.

Dalmatia's most southerly islands of Mljet, the Elaphiti islands, and Lokrum, as well as the Pelješac peninsula, offer adventurous swimmers unique options, such as the beaches by the city walls of Dubrovnik and the coves just before the border to Montenegro.

The south of Croatia

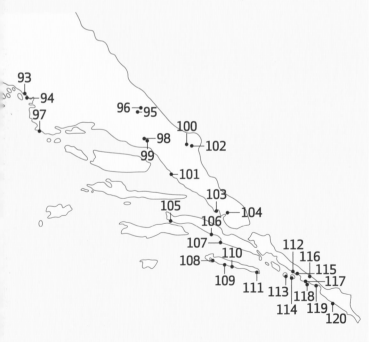

ALMOST A LITTLE SPOOKY –
Šibenik submarine bunker

The Šibenik Channel, which connects the Bay of Sibenik with the Adriatic Sea, is approx. 2km long and in parts only between 140 and 220m wide. Due to the tightness of this busy shipping lane it is prohibited to drop anchor and swim here. This makes wild swimming for individuals much more difficult.

However, there is an alternative. Slovenian long-distance swimmer Martin Strel, who swam the Amazon, amongst many other rivers, runs "Strel Swimming Adventure Holidays" and offers a legal swimming experience in what is a 250m-long and 15m-deep tunnel. Like most of the other submarine bunkers, the aptly named Hitler's Eye was built by the Germans during World War II and subsequently used by the Yugoslav Army for another 50 years. Further attractions of the Šibenik Channel include the Cave of Saint Anthony, near the bunker, and the St Nicholas Fort, at the entrance into the channel.

→ **Directions:**
For further information please visit: www.strel-swimming.com or www.schwimmferien.ch.

→ **GPS:** 43.72729, 15.87421

Cave of Saint Anthony

St Nicholas Fort

SALINE SPA –
Veliko jezero, Šibenik

The coastal village of Zablaće, 8km from Šibenik, has been home to the families of salt workers, for which Šibenik has been known since the Middle Ages, over many hundreds of years. During Ottoman campaigns, the village was completely destroyed on two occasions. Eventually, salt production was abandoned and the inhabitants changed the way in which they earned their living first to cattle farming, then to agriculture and, more recently, to tourism.

Many of the residents became well-regarded seamen or emigrated to America.

Today, the Veliko jezero ("Big Lake") and the Mala Solina ("Small Saline") are the last surviving remnants of the time of salt production. Both are located on a peninsula south of the Šibenik Channel and are best circumnavigated and explored by bicycle. With respect to the clarity and depth of the water, both bodies of water are no swimming revelation but are rather shallow and muddy. However, it is precisely this mud that has now been recognised as having healing properties for the treatment of rheumatic illnesses. Well, if it helps, who can argue with that…

→ **Directions:**
Exit the E65 motorway at Vrpolje. At the first crossroads, turn right onto Route 58 and follow the road through Donje Polje until you can see a big shopping mall. Just before the mall, turn left onto Route 8, then turn into the first road on your right. Shortly afterwards, turn left and follow the road until the saline appears on your right. Then turn into the second road on your right.

→ **GPS:** 43.7089, 15.88334

MILLS BY THE RUSHING STREAM –
Grab

Sinjsko polje is a karst area in the Dalmatian hinterland, the so-called Zagora. It is a highly fertile area of more than 60km2 of karst land where wheat and maize have been grown since ancient times. If one adds to this the region's abundance of water it makes perfect sense that the area was a centre of the milling industry. This also applies to the river Grab, whose hydro-power becomes usable immediately after its ice-cold water leaves the source pool, located below a rocky ridge. Then the stream flows towards the Ruda and Cetina.

Today, two adjacent mills are still in operation on the river Grab (a) and are in great demand by local farmers. Both millers are friendly and welcoming and keen to show visitors the remarkable site with its century-old and proven milling process. It is possible to swim both in the weir area and in a few pools upstream of the mills, or in the source of the Grab which is only a few hundred metres away.

→ **Directions:**

Exit the E65 motorway at Bisko and follow Route 60, direction Trilj. Before you reach the village of Jabuka turn left into the Grab valley. In the village of Grab itself, turn right to the upper reaches of the Grab and park by the "Waterfall House". From here, follow the trail on the right towards the mill and along the river to the spring.

→ **GPS:** 43.64362, 16.76542

A PURE SOURCE OF ENERGY –
Ruda

The spring of the river Ruda is a mighty source pool. A short distance downstream, its water cascades through a gorge before forming a waterfall by an old mill. This spot served as a location for the German-produced Western *The Oil Prince*, and the romantic spring has rightly been declared a nature reserve. The limestone cliffs of the gorge, which are densely overgrown by scrub, are home to rare bird species, and the immediate environment of the spring provides shelter for various reptiles and amphibians. In addition, endemic fish species find an ideal habitat in the source pool.

While swimming here is only advisable for those with a hardy constitution, a bath in the spring (a) or main current or outflowing leat of the mill (b) will be refreshing and energising. Downstream of the mill, by the water, tables and benches allow you to sit in reverie or enjoy the perfect picnic.

→ **Directions:**
Exit the E65 motorway at Bisko and follow Route 60, direction Trilj. Before you get to the village of Jabuka, turn left into the Grab valley. Once you are in the village of Grab itself, turn left, direction Vrabač, and continue to Ruda. Park by the mill. The spring is immediately upstream of the mill.

→ **GPS:** 43.66876, 16.79301

WHEN THE DRAGON AWAKES –

Dragon Eye's Lake (Zmajevo oko)

This "geo-hydromorphological phenomenon" is connected to countless legends, myths and fairy tales, as well as being the subject of various scientific theories. The lake is surrounded by 4-to-24m-tall rocks that, exercising great caution, can be used for cliff-diving. Although the lake has no obvious connection to the sea, which is only about 150m away, tidal changes of the water table are detectable. Every 30 years or so, the "dragon" awakes. During this extraordinary event, which has only been explained very recently, the lake "boils". This means that a layer of hydrogen sulphide, which usually rests in deeper layers of water, pushes to the lake's surface, thereby preventing any oxygen supply to the water and subsequently resulting in the

death of all living organisms in the lake. The last such event occurred in 1997. A few months later, the lake miraculously resumes its clear appearance and life slowly returns to the water. Bearing this knowledge in mind, swimming in the Dragon Eye's Lake might not be everyone's cup of tea. Some swimmers feel that the water has a strange sulphuric quality. Whether that's a figment of their imagination or not, who can say? Without dwelling any further on theory, swimming here is an unforgettable experience, and if you feel the need you can make the short journey to the sea afterwards to "cleanse" yourself from any funny smells!

→ **Directions:**
Approaching from Trogir, follow Route 8, direction Primošten. Take the turning to Rogoznica and follow the signs to Marina Frapa. Use the big car park by the port. From there, the walk to the lake takes only a few minutes.

→ **GPS:** 43.53055, 15.95908

BATHING FUN IN A FORMER PRINCIPALITY –
Stružica

Trnbusi once belonged to the legendary tiny Principality (or Republic) of Poljica that, over centuries, had to defend itself against Ottoman invasions. Then, as now, Trnbusi is on the river Cetina, which marked the border to the Ottoman Empire from the 16th to the 18th century.

The Cetina meanders in the Trnbusi parish area. At moderate speed, it flows through one of its countless canyons before opening up into a slightly wider valley upstream of Blato na Cetini.

Upstream of a small weir-like structure, the locals have created a beautiful river bathing spot called Stružica. It is easy to reach by car and includes a sunbathing lawn and diving board.

To demonstrate that they haven't lost any of their vigour and spirit, the former "Policijans" hold the traditional annual New Year's Swim in the 6°C water of the river Cetina, in absolutely freezing conditions.

→ **Directions:**
Exit the E65 motorway at Blato na Cetini and follow Route 70 to the signposted village. Before you get to the bridge, turn left and, after approx. 1.5km, turn right into a track to the beach.

→ **GPS:** 43.4898, 16.81629

FAMILY SPOT WITH A MILL –
Blato on Cetina

There is hardly any other river in Croatia which offers such a wide variety of different wild swimming spots. However, some of these spots along the seductive river Cetina are unsuitable for families or are very difficult to access. This spot by the Cetina bridge in Blato na Cetini is quite different and not at all muddy. In Croatian, "Blato" means mud or swamp, which doesn't sound promising, but actually the spot is beautifully clean. As is often the case, this is another spot where the site of an old mill provides wild swimming joy, and in this case extremely family-friendly.

An easy-to-walk track on the right-hand bank directly by the bridge leads to a nice sunbathing lawn with ample shade provided by old trees. Close to the bank, on the inside of the river bend, the water is shallow and the current is moderate, which means that bathing here is safe, even for small children. As an adult, swimming gets better when you wade a little towards the outside of the bend where you can swim against the river's current. Please note that this spot doesn't have any facilities.

→ **Directions:**
Exit the E65 motorway at Blato na Cetini and follow Route 70 to the signposted village. Park ahead of the bridge and take the trail to the right, passing through the mill, to the bathing spot.

→ **GPS:** 43.47939, 16.84599

TWO UNIQUE, SPRING-FED POOLS –
Dva Oka

"Two Eyes" is the telling name of these two small, spring-fed pools of the river Vrljika in Imotski Krajina, one of the most interesting regions of the Dalmatian hinterland, the Zagora. Here, in a very small area, a multitude of different forms of craters can be found that are like almost nothing else in Europe.

These utterly beautiful, but icy-cold blue "eyes" have an approximate diameter of 40m and a depth of 10m. They are the most glittering representatives of the five sources of the Vrijlka,

a karst stream that carries water throughout the year and eventually runs into the periodic lake Prolosko Blato.

The upper reaches of the Vrijlka are home to numerous endangered animal species, such as the Dalmatian minnow and a rare species of river crab. From the two spring lakes you can walk to the "Green Dome", a pilgrimage church where every year, on 15th August, the feast day of Mary's Assumption is celebrated with a big procession.

→ **Directions:**
From E65 motorway (exit Zagvozd) take Route 76 to Grubine. Follow Route 60 and take the turning to Donji Proložac. Park by the small Catholic church of Crkva Velike Gospe and take the hiking trail leading north.

→ **GPS:** 43.45667, 17.17516

OUT OF MAKARSKA –
Nugal beach

Over the course of its long history, Makarska was ruled by the Romans, Ottomans, Bosnians, Venetians, Habsburgs and Croats. Today, it is not foreign powers but whole armies of tourists who occupy this lively town at the Riviera of the same name during the summer months. The Biokovo mountain range towers above the town. It can be reached by car on a mountain road from which you can enjoy terrific views far across the Adriatic Sea. Popular beaches start right by the town's seafront but the best-known of them are located slightly outside town.

Nugal beach is predominantly visited by nudists. It is approx. 2km from the harbour, between the towns of Makarska and Tučepi, and is regarded as one of Croatia's most beautiful beaches. The beach is only accessible on foot or by boat. Its shoreline is made of fine, white gravel and the cove is embedded into an amphitheatre of rocks. There is a shady pinewood and the fabulous blue sea with mesmerising hues of turquoise and blues. Even a small waterfall flows into the cove that, up to now, has been spared any form of tourist infrastructure.

→ **Directions:**
Turn off the S8 coastal road and park by the harbour. On foot, the woodland trail through the Osejava Park to the beach takes about 30 minutes.

→ **GPS:** 43.27938, 17.03392

THE DEEP BLUE
Blue Lake

The sights of the village of Imotski include the old town, which was built on terraces, as well as the mediaeval castle and the football stadium, constructed in a sinkhole. But the undisputed star amongst them, and very close by, is the "Blue Lake". This moody beauty spans a whole range of possibilities. At high water, the lake allegedly has a depth of 100m, a figure hard to imagine, whereas in the autumn it often dries up completely. The latter situation is put to good use by the village's residents, who hold their traditional football match at the bottom of the absent lake, employing a highly original set of rules.

As early as the end of the 19th century, gravel tracks were laid down the steep cauldron. In high summer, these tracks are open to the public for a small fee (no charge being applied during the rest of the year), thereby allowing you a unique swimming experience, provided that the water level is sufficient. Not suitable for swimming, but definitely worth seeing, is the so-called "Red Lake" in a 500m-deep sinkhole approx. 1.5km from the Blue Lake. This sinkhole is one of the largest in the world and the Red Lake fills it to about half of its depth.

→ **Directions:**
Exit the E65 motorway at Zagvozd and follow Route 76 to Grubine. Then take Route 60 to Imotski. In the village, follow the signs to Modro Jezero and park below the fortress. The steep descent to the lake takes about 20 minutes.

→ **GPS:** 43.45381, 17.21545

JUST ABOVE SEA LEVEL, AND ALSO BELOW IT –
Baćina lakes

Neatly lined up, like blue and green pearls on a necklace, Ocuša, Crniševo, Podgora, Sladinac, Vrbnik and Plitko are six of a total of seven Baćina lakes. All of them are close to the port town of Ploče, situated between the delta of the river Neretva, the sea and the coastal mountains. Anglers, biologists and botanists alike are ecstatic about these lagoon-like lakes with their brackish water, covering a total area of 20km2 at depths of 5 to 50m.

The lakes have formed in true cryptodepressions and as a result their surface is a mere 80cm above sea level, while their bottom reaches far below it. The lakes are predominantly fed by two springs: one fresh-water spring in Lake Ocša and a saltwater spring in Lake Crniševo. Their variable flows and the enormous catchment area result in the lakes' heavily fluctuating water levels. The lakes are also prone to flooding. You can find the best bathing spots on the southern shore and the more remote western shore of the main lake, which is close to the road.

→ **Directions:**
Route 8 leads past the western edge of the lakes, between Ploče and Gradac. Access to the lakes is from a hill near a war memorial and is well signposted.

→ **GPS:** 43.07034, 17.4212

Despite being an intensely farmed region, the valley of the lower reaches of the river Neretva is pretty and highly biodiverse. For waterbirds, in particular, it is a real paradise, not least due to its enormous frog population.

Modro Oko, or "Blue Eye", is part of a sunken karst slab on the right bank of the Neretva, between Desne, Banja and Komin. This sinkhole, which is roughly at sea level, is about 20m deep and connected to the lake of Desne by a small canal. The slightly salty water of the Blue Eye gets its radiant blue colour from its high limestone content. Swimming is basically only possible from the western shore by the remnants of a derelict building. If you feel hungry afterwards, you can try the culinary speciality of the Neretva valley: "Brodet", a frog and eel casserole. This hearty feast is served in the inns of the nearby villages.

→ **Directions:**
Turn off Route 8 by the bridge over the Neretva. Drive along the right bank of the wide canal, up until the turning to Banja and Desne, until you can see the "Blue Eye" on your right, below the road. Park the car by the roadside and walk down to the lake. This should only take a few minutes.

→ **GPS:** 43.06385, 17.51007

EXTREMELY EXTRAVAGANT –
Duba cove

Pelješac is Croatia's second-largest peninsula. It is 65km long and stretches almost parallel to the Adriatic coast between the fortress town of Ston in the south and Cape Lovište in the north. Apart from its beautiful bays, coves and beaches, many of which can only be reached by four-wheel-drive or boat, the peninsula is known for its mussels and olives, but most of all for its wine. To get to one of the most amazing coves of Pelješac, north-west of Lovište, you have to face a rather adventurous rough track.

It is most likely due to this difficult access that Duba cove has retained its peaceful and quiet atmosphere, even in peak season. Its uncrowded beach is definitely not due to a lack of attractiveness because this small cove is simply superb! Surrounded by pine woods, it presents a beach of fine, white gravel and a breathtakingly blue sea with awesome views of the opposite island of Korčula. In the cove, an old fisherman's cottage has been lovingly restored and is now the family-owned Konoba Estravaganca, a tavern that exclusively serves fresh fish and seafood, among them the famous Ston mussels.

→ **Directions:**
Turn off the (coastal) Route 8 and head for the Pelješac peninsula. Stay on Route 414, passing Ston and Orebić, direction Lovište. Shortly before you reach Lovište, which is the most northerly village on the peninsula, turn left and, sticking to a wild rough track, follow the sign to Restaurant Estravaganca.

→ **GPS:** 43.00253, 17.0381

THE ROAD, THROUGH VINEYARDS, TO HEAVEN –
Pijavičino cove

The sunny slopes above this swimming spot are ideal for growing some of the finest wines in the world. Typical for this region of Croatia is Postup with its purple to dark red colour. It has a high alcohol content and is produced from the Plavac Mali grape, an ancient autochthonous red wine variety from Croatia's southern islands. Many of these wines can be tested on-site without any obligation to purchase the product. The restaurants also offer white wines, which are the preferred choice with the island's famous mussel recipes.

Up until now, there were no permanent residents in this marvellous cove. However, we spotted a building site here in late summer 2020, which could indicate that this blissful situation is about to change. Even if the cove doesn't have any beach as such, its location is simply divine. The stone jetty provides a flat surface for your beach towel as well as offering easy access to the water. It is good fun swimming out to the small rocky outcrop offshore.

→ **Directions:**
Turn off the (coastal) Route 8 and head for the Pelješac peninsula. Stay on Route 414, passing Ston, until you get to the wine-growing village of Potomje. There, turn left, through the Dingač tunnel. Then turn left again and always keep left until you get to a sharp right bend. From here, follow the road to the cove.

→ **GPS:** 42.913, 17.36658

ESCAPE TO THE ISLAND –
Vučine cove

The tiny fishing village of Žuljana on the south-west shore of the Pelješac peninsula has only 200 inhabitants and offers mesmerising views of the island of Mljet and the Mljet Channel. Here you can also enjoy the Dingač, a full-bodied red wine that is grown in sea-facing vineyards and takes a very long time to fully mature.

The small Kremena beach is to the north of the village, whereas Vučine beach, being significantly larger and more family-friendly, is to the south. This gently sloping gravel-and-sand beach is flanked by beautiful pine forest that stretches almost to the sea. The cove has a small restaurant, which is only open in high summer, and Portaloos. It is truly enchanting to swim across to a small island, a distance of about 800m, and be on your own desert island – just for a while.

→ **Directions:**
   Turn off the (coastal) Route 8 and head for the Pelješac peninsula. Stay on Route 414 to Dubrava. There, turn left to Žuljana. Vučine cove is behind a small hill south of the village.

→ **GPS:** 42.88591, 17.45114

Offshore island

View from the island to the cove

INDEFINITE SWIMMING IN THE SALTWATER LAKE –

Veliko jezero, Mljet

Around 10,000 years ago, the inland region, which today is within the National Park of the island of Mljet, sank, and two basins were formed as a result. The Veliko jezero ("Big Lake") and Malo jezero ("Small Lake") are connected not just to each other but also to the sea, which feeds it with salt water. These narrow channels, which are spanned by elegant bridges, have currents that are strong enough for driving watermills in days gone by. Today, these natural counter-current facilities allow you to swim "indefinitely" in the same spot. This works better by the big modern bridge than by the small mediaeval one.

Please note that within the National Park you may only swim in designated bathing spots that are shown on a map. One of these spots is on the monastery island in the "Big Lake". This bathing spot, like all other stops on the "Veliko jezero", is reached by a pleasure boat that crosses the lake at regular intervals. You can also hike around both lakes on a 12km-long tour and marvel at the fabulous views, the aromatic scent of the Mediterranean flora, and glorious holm oak and pine forests.

→ **Directions:**
  Take the car ferry from Prapratno on the Plješac peninsula to cross the Adriatic Sea to Sobra ferry port on Mljet. Follow Route 120, direction Pomena, until you get to the signs for the car park by the lake. From here, the walk to the tourist information centre and the pleasure boat's departure point takes approx. 5 minutes.

→ **GPS:** 42.76852, 17.37485

SUNSET BEACH –
Sutmholjska beach

Like all other beaches on Mljet, this one in the centre of the island also has crystal-clear and clean water. In the middle section of the cove, the beach consists of fine gravel and sand, while the sides offer great spaces for sunbathing on flat slabs of rock. Due to its south-westerly orientation and the wide expanse of the horizon, this cove is known for its spectacular sunsets.

During the day, a small pinewood provides protection from too much sun. You can get drinks and snacks from a small beach restaurant. Occasionally, in high summer, a small parking charge is applied, but access to the beach via steep steps is generally free. A popular way to get to the beach is to rent one of the numerous hire scooters that are available everywhere on the island. The nearby Camp Mungos offers further catering and entertainment options.

→ **Directions:**
Take the car ferry from Prapratno on the Plješac peninsula to cross the Adriatic Sea to Sobra ferry port on Mljet. Follow Route 120 through Babino Polje and then take the second road on the left to get to the beach.

→ **GPS:** 42.74184, 17.49915

LEGENDARY LOVE NEST –
Odysseus's Cave

Many islands in the Mediterranean Sea, including Mljet, claim to be among those visited by Odysseus, hero of Homer's epics, during his Odyssey. On Mljet, the claim is underpinned and geographically "nailed down" by Odysseus's Cave on the island's south coast. This is a karst cave flooded by the sea whose roof has collapsed. Just offshore is a rock called "Ogiran", named after the legendary cliff that caused Odysseus's ship to be wrecked. At high tide or when there is a strong southerly wind, the submerged rock is hardly visible, posing a serious danger to seafarers.

It is said that Odysseus was stranded in this very spot but found shelter in the cave. According to legend, he was initially nursed back to health by the nymph Calypso but ended up being held against his will by this beautiful creature of the sea who had fallen in love with him. One thing, however, is certain: up until the 19th century, the cave was home to monk seals, a species that once thrived in the Mediterranean.

→ **Directions:**
Take the car ferry from Prapratno on the Plješac peninsula to cross the Adriatic Sea to Sobra ferry port on Mljet. Follow Route 120 to Babino Polje and park by the Tommy Supermarket. The signposted walk to the coast takes about 30 minutes.

→ **GPS:** 42.72945, 17.54399

COLLECTING MUSHROOMS IS PROHIBITED! –
Mala Saplunara

Legend has it that Odysseus spent quite some time on the island of Mljet, and also came to this beautiful cove. It is the habitat of an extremely rare and therefore strictly protected species of beach mushroom, although it is unlikely that these would have been the reason for Odysseus's visit. However, there are also many other qualities that this protected nature reserve has to offer.

For example, the water temperature in the sheltered and shallow sandy cove can reach up to 28°C in summer. Also, the quality of the water is exquisite. This excellent and easy-to-access beach is extremely family-friendly and has been rated as a Blue Flag beach. Behind the 1km-long cove, which is divided into a "Big" and a "Small" Saplunara, is a pinewood where you can find shade. In high summer, the beach has a café with deckchair hire, Portaloos and a coin-operated shower. A small car park in the wood has space for about 20 cars.

→ **Directions:**
Take the car ferry from Prapratno on the PljEšac peninsula to cross the Adriatic Sea to Sobra ferry port on Mljet. Follow Route 123 to Saplunara and drive through the village and past Velika Suplanara until you get to Mala Suplanara cove.

→ **GPS:** 42.69633, 17.74108

"THE GOOD WATER" –
Brana

When the plague devastated the land in the 16th century, a poor old man from Orašac, a mountain hamlet near Dubrovnik, had a vision one night of St Mary. She told him that if the residents were able to build her a church by the Spring of Good Water the village would be spared any future recurrence of plague, famine or war. The building project was welcomed by the people, sufficient funds were raised, and from the very day that the foundation stone was laid the Black Death became a thing of the past.

A few centuries later, a reservoir was constructed above the church that dammed the Good Water to irrigate the region's fruit groves. Today, this tiny Brana reservoir, from whose dam there are the most marvellous views of the sea, is also great for bathing and angling. There is an astonishing custom connected with the lake: during carnival, in secrecy, one of the village's fishing boats is "transferred" from the sea to the lake at night. The boat is only returned to its rightful home when the unfortunate owner has laid on a generous feast for the villagers.

→ **Directions:**
From Route 5, in the village of Orašac, drive up a steep, narrow lane by the bakery until you get to the wider high street. Here, turn left and continue until you see the sign for the church. Turn right, park by the church and walk a few minutes to the reservoir's dam.

→ **GPS:** 42.70282, 18.01311

GOLDEN BEACH ON A GREEN ISLAND –
Šunj

Day-trippers from Dubrovnik love the Elaphiti islands, and Lopud in particular. It is one of the least populated of these islands and, due to a good supply of fresh water, also the greenest. "Green" applies in other ways as well, since there is no traffic on the 4.5km2 island, apart from a few bicycles, scooters and golf buggies. Instead, you will find many lush gardens and parks.

Roughly 1.5km of the 12km-long coastline are covered by sandy beaches. The village of Lopud is located in a sandy cove, which is rare given that the island's north-west side is predominantly rocky. From the village, a track leads between two hills and past a large number of chapels and churches to Bišun cove on the opposite side of the island. Allegedly, Bišun is derived from the Italian word for snake (*biscione*). Today, this golden sandy beach is called Šunj and is very popular with sailors and other seafarers.

→ **Directions:**
Sail from Dubrovnik or the nearer Zaton by pleasure boat, chartered boat or your own boat.

→ **GPS:** 42.67949, 17.95157

EXPLORING SEA CAVES –
Koločep island

The Greeks named this most southerly island of the Elaphites "Kalomata", which is derived from the Greek term "kalos", meaning beautiful. Koločep has retained its name until this day, and local people are proud of its ancient history. Despite having larger coves such as Saplura and Porat with sandy and gravel beaches, Koločep is predominantly known for its rocky coast, with secret caves and countless options for cliff-diving. For example, by the lighthouse is a small rock pool from which you can swim underwater to the open sea. You can also risk a 5m dive into the pool from the surrounding rocks. Of course, there are many cliffs that are considerably higher.

The other sea caves, which you can swim into from the sea, are only accessible by boat. At normal swell, swimming into the caves is quite easy and you don't need to dive to get to them. Highly popular is the "Blue Cave" (b), a favourite destination for numerous pleasure boats from Dubrovnik. Further to the west are the "Three Caves" (a). Of these, the one to the very right is the most interesting because it is safe to swim through it, re-emerging on the other side of what is a tiny cape.

→ **Directions:**
Travel from Dubrovnik or the nearer Zaton by pleasure boat, chartered boat or your own boat.

→ **GPS:** a) 42.67186, 17.99761, b) 42.66357, 18.01629

b)

b)

a)

SIMPLY BEAUTIFUL –
Zaton

Broadly speaking, "Zaton" is a cove in English. Together, Veliki Zaton and Mali Zaton, in conjunction with two smaller hamlets, constitute the parish of Zaton to the north-west of Dubrovnik. The various parts of the community, which are scattered across the small bay, are connected by a beachfront promenade that is perfect for a stroll by the seaside. Veliki Zaton has a small beach of rough gravel, a pier and a few bars and restaurants. However, more remote and more beautiful are the two rocky coves at the cape that can be reached on pretty tracks through a pine forest.

The rope, which is attached in this spot, has led to it being given the name "Tarzan Cove" (a). From this bathing spot, steep concrete steps lead down to the tiny gap in the rocks. There is also a small jetty that serves as a diving board for jumping into the deep, crystal-clear water. For sunbathing, on the other hand, the upper platform by the beginning of the steps is more suitable. Gof beach (b) has a rock pool that is somewhat separated from the open sea, and here the sea is calmer and the water warmer. Watching the sunset from this cove is a wonderful experience!

→ **Directions:**
Tarzan Cove is accessible by walking from Veliki Zaton along the shoreline in the direction of the cape. If you continue on the track around the cape and past a small beacon, you get to a chapel and cemetery. Soon afterwards, a steep track leads down to Gof cove.

→ **GPS:** a) 42.68511, 18.0455
b) 42.68651, 18.03877

It is open for discussion as to whether this karst river, which is only a 5km linear distance from the city centre of Dubrovnik, is just 20m or indeed 4.2km long. Mostly, the Ombla is perceived as a bay of the Adriatic Sea which is spanned by the distinctive Franjo Tudman Bridge and also includes Dubrovnik's Gruž port that is suitable for small boats.

The source of the Ombla is a lively karst spring in a big cave. Merely 20m downstream of where the spring emerges is a weir. Fresh water is a precious commodity in this part of the world, and the Ombla has been used for supplying Dubrovnik with drinking water since 1437 AD. This area is therefore fenced off and cannot be entered. Below the weir, near the old disused waterworks, a section of the Ombla begins that is influenced by the sea and where swimming is allowed. On the opposite bank, by the river, is a bar where you can also enter the water, which is wonderfully refreshing even in high summer.

→ **Directions:**
  On the city-facing side of the Tudman Bridge, take the exit towards Sustjepan/ACI Marina Dubrovnik. When you get to the next bridge, which spans the river in a semi-circle, continue straight ahead and park by the old waterworks. In summer, you may want to choose the bar on the opposite riverbank to access the water.

→ **GPS:** 42.67509, 18.13679

WHAT A STUNNING SETTING! –
Dubrovnik's beaches by the city walls

In 1979, the Old Town of Dubrovnik became one of the UNESCO's World Heritage sites. Particularly impressive are the old city walls that have served as a location for *Game of Thrones* but that are also known for two of the most unusual beaches of this city. Buža beach (a) nestles on the southern city wall between white limestone rocks that form level platforms and steep steps that lead down to the sea. The cliffs are ideal for diving into the deep blue water. A small bar plays music and serves chilled drinks.

Porporela (b), at the eastern end of the city wall, is not just the best-known part of the Old Town but also one of the most popular beaches with Dubrovnik's residents. From Porporela you get a fabulous view of the island of Lokrum. Also, one can try out a game of water polo or simply marvel at the most fantastic sunsets.

→ **Directions:**
   a) Behind the Cathedral of Dubrovnik is a small door from where a set of stairs leads to the bathing platforms in the rocks.
   b) At the small pier, where the pleasure vessels to Lokrum depart, keep to the right and follow the city wall.

→ **GPS:** a) 42.63881, 18.10871, b) 42.63975, 18.11275

a)

b)

b)

LIVELY ISLAND WITH A "DEAD SEA" –
Lokrum

Lokrum is only 650m away from the Old Town of Dubrovnik. From May to October, frequent regular boat services connect the city with this small island. Lokrum is a nature reserve and a popular destination for local people and tourists alike, with a good number of sights, events and entertainment venues. The monastery ruin was a location for *Game of Thrones* and the botanical garden, which was opened in 1959, is home to more than 800 plant species. The island's coastline offers many beautiful bathing spots.

On Lokrum's south side, which can be reached via one of the many footpaths, is the small salt lake of Mrtvo More (meaning "Dead Sea") (a). The lake is surrounded on three sides by tall rocks, but one side is easily accessible. This beach side has a café with a lovely lounge. The "Dead Sea" is connected to the open sea by an underground passage and displays a high salt content, hence its name.

The slightly less steep eastern side of the island has one official beach (b), as well as many unofficial nudist beaches.

→ **Directions:**
   Make the passage with a pleasure boat from Dubrovnik. On the island itself, you can get around using the well-signposted footpaths.

→ **GPS:** a) 42.62259, 18.1204, b) 42.62272, 18.12642

b)

a)

b)

A "LOST" PLACE THAT GIVES FOOD FOR THOUGHT –
Kupari cove

In centuries past, Dubrovnik's characteristic red roofing tiles were produced by the Kuparica factory in Kupari (*"kupa"* = roof tile). Suffering the same fate as Dubrovnik and many other villages in the south of Croatia, the once flourishing resort of Kupari (where Tito, the former president of Yugoslavia, had a villa) was severely damaged by troops from Serbia and Montenegro during the Yugoslav Wars.

Legendary hotels on the beautiful beach of Župa Dubrovačka, such as the Grand Hotel Kupari, Hotel Pelegrin and Hotel Goricina, were all looted, shelled and set on fire. There have been efforts in recent years to revive the area. Rumour has it that, in 2020, investors joined forces to develop a large-scale resort. Until that happens, you can still explore this bizarre and attractive place in peace, and enjoy the wonderful sea.

→ **Directions:**
   From Dubrovnik, follow Route 8 to Kupari. In the centre of the village, ahead of the petrol station, turn right to the beach.

→ **GPS:** 42.61996, 18.19146

Pasjača beach

ALMOST IN MONTENEGRO –
Pasjača beach

This beach near the hamlet of Popovići, close to the border with Montenegro, is breathtaking in two respects: firstly, because of its natural beauty, and secondly because it can only be reached via a steep trail that has been blown into the rocky coast with the help of explosives. Please be aware that children, in particular, after a long and tiring day on this beach, might find the return journey uphill back to the car park exhausting.

It is due to this, and also the fact that this stretch of coastline is rather unsuitable for dropping anchor, that there is a good chance that during peak season you will not need to share this gem of a beach with many other bathers. Its red-spotted rocks, the white gravel and the bright blue sea make Pasjača one of the most photogenic beaches in Croatia. Please note that you will need to provide shade and catering yourself as there are no facilities. Along the trail, you can admire the fishermen's "boat shelters" high up in the rock face.

→ **Directions:**
From Dubrovnik, follow Route 8 southbound towards the border. Shortly before you get to the border, at the signpost to Popoviči, turn right and drive through the hamlet. Park in a small car park on the cliffs and then take the steep footpath down to the cove.

→ **GPS:** 42.51166, 18.32295

THE CETINA

A RIVER BOTH LOVED AND FEARED BY MOUNTAIN FARMERS AND PIRATES ALIKE

From its source area on the north-west slopes of the mighty Dinara mountain range to the former privateers' nest by the river's mouth at Omiš, this moody river has both fascinated and frightened the region's residents over the centuries. When its eight springs, among them the powerful and mysterious Glasevo spring, disgorged vast quantities of water, the river valley was threatened by devastating floods. Therefore, people have attempted to tame this wild beauty since ancient times. Today, the gigantic Peruća reservoir on the young river Cetina gives testimony to these efforts. It is a sign of the times that the enormous energy potential of the Cetina is these days less utilised by watermills and more by hydropower stations.

After the Cetina has passed the Peruća reservoir its course runs through a karst region. Then it irrigates the fields around Sinj and finally swirls through a narrow rocky canyon below Nutjak fort. Such fortifications primarily served as protection against raids by the Turks, since the Cetina marked the border with the Ottoman Empire for several centuries. At Zadvarje, the river has created its most impressive canyon, and also Dalmatia's tallest waterfall, the 50m Gubavica fall. From there, the Cetina changes its course towards the west and, after one hundred eventful kilometres, it flows into the Adriatic Sea at Omiš. Apart from its huge importance for agriculture and power generation, the Cetina is also intensely utilised by adventure tourism. There is hardly any other river that can provide such unforgettable hikes, canyoning and boat trips, and wild-swimming experiences as the alluring Cetina.

WORTH SEEING BUT NOT FOR SWIMMING

Zelenci – one of the sources of the Save

Virje waterfall at Bovec

Martuljek falls, Kranska Gora

Waterfalls can be tricky things. In addition to their plunge pool having to be both deep enough and big enough, the water level also needs to be just right. Furthermore, there are many falls that are worth seeing but, because of their shape and form, are unsuitable from a swimmer's perspective. Examples of waterfalls that are at best suited for showering but won't allow for even a dip include the Peričnik, Martuljek and Kropa falls, to name just a few. It is, however, beyond doubt that these falls and many others are worth visiting simply for their attractiveness as wonders of the natural world. Apart from that, there are marvellous (karst) phenomena that would tempt any wild-swimming enthusiast but that are rightly protected because of their particular fragile ecology. These include the idyllic source of the Save at Zelenci and the water-bearing Škocjan and Cross caves.

In addition, a few spots where swimming had been legal have recently had swimming bans imposed. Examples are the Skradinski Buk in the Krka National Park and the idyllic Virje waterfall in Bovec. These swimming bans were not introduced because the bathing spots are too dangerous, or because swimming would have caused significant damage, but because large numbers of people have partied there, making a lot of noise, playing loud music and leaving rubbish and broken glass behind. True wild swimmers they certainly were not. It is in all of our interest to always enjoy bathing spots responsibly and carefully, leaving them more spotless than we found them in the first place.

WORTH SEEING BUT
NOT FOR SWIMMING

Peričnik waterfall, Triglav National Park

By the Škocjan caves

Skradinski Buk, Krka National Park

IS IT ALL A QUESTION OF TIMING?

WHERE THERE WAS WATER ONCE, WATER WILL RETURN

Being in the right place at the right time frequently makes the difference between wild-swimming fun and wild-swimming disappointment. And seasonal forecasts are not always correct. Whereas you can generally assume that most inland bodies of water will have their highest water levels from spring to early summer, there are always exceptions to the rule, and surprises. For example, on a late summer tour, when there should be very little water in Slovenian or Croatian waterfalls, you might find that the opposite is the case and that some spots are unsuitable for swimming because of high water levels. Forecasts are particularly difficult for karst springs and rivers, with their underground watercourses. Heavy rainfall in a faraway valley is often enough to make a spring that has been merely a damp patch turn into a prolific fountain. On the other hand, the fact that a particular body of water is carrying water right now is no guarantee that you will find the same conditions nearby. With wild water, good and bad luck are often not far apart.

SOONER OR LATER ALL WILL BE WELL

Naturally, those who don't need to travel when everybody else is travelling are better off. Hundreds of people on a beach that you thought was off the beaten track and would be nice and quiet might well impair your experience of nature. To make sure that you can enjoy your favourite spots even during peak season, it is best to plan your visit for around the beginning or end of the day. The "early bird" will have a more intense swimming experience. Also, a sundowner doesn't always have to be an alcoholic drink: swimming into the sunset is always very special. At times, even during peak season, it can be sufficient to simply walk a few steps further from the crowd, to remain flexible, and to aim for the nameless cove next door or the spot around the next corner that isn't quite as easy to reach.

ASSESSING THE SITUATION

"HANG ON..."

"The guidebook says that swimming is allowed here.."
Situations, conditions and property rights can change
at any time. From one day to the next, swimming can be
prohibited and the very bathing spot that was safe today
can become dangerous tomorrow. Many descriptions
are mere snapshots in time. Even the best travel guides
and the most precise descriptions cannot remain valid
indefinitely, and nothing can replace one's own sense
of responsibility and common sense. Therefore, please
make sure that you check the situation on-site on a
particular day before taking unnecessary risks. There's
got to be time for that!

PACKRAFTS –
BOATS MADE FOR WILD SWIMMING

PACK WHAT?

"Packraft" is a newly coined word that combines the terms "backpacking" and "rafting". These watercraft are also called "backpack boats". The "raft" bit can be confusing because the term raft is also used for big dinghies with a crew of several people that are used for heavy-duty whitewater rafting.

BACKPACK BOATS THAT PUT UP WITH ANYTHING

Packrafts are air-filled travel boats that are characterised by their lightweight and compact dimensions while being extremely robust at the same time. The accessories, such as paddles and air pump, are also optimised in terms of weight and size. The paddles are collapsible into several parts (up to four) and are often made of carbon. Instead of the conventional air pump or bellows, an extremely light "air bag" is used. Smaller boats can even be inflated by mouth. This kind of kit is ideal for hiking or bike tours. Of course, it is also suited for wild-swimming use.

THE BIG ADVANTAGES OF THESE LIGHTWEIGHT BOATS

Packrafts are easy to store, both at home and in the car, on public transport or in your hiking backpack. The most compact versions allow you to transport the entire boat equipment in a swim buoy or a SWACK, which has been co-developed and improved by me and is a combination of a hiking backpack and swim buoy.

When one combines all of these pieces of equipment, it is possible to put together interesting, mixed hiking, paddling and swimming tours. For example, you walk along the upper reaches of a river, carrying the boat equipment in the SWACK. Having reached the entry point, take the boat equipment out of the backpack and sail the shallower upper reaches of the wild river with the packraft. As soon as you get to the lower reaches of the stream or river, where swimming is possible, you can store the boat equipment in the SWACK and now use the SWACK as a swim buoy. The SWACK is inflated and the swimmer pulls it behind them, connected to a waist belt. This will not impair the swimming style. Despite the added weight, the "swim buoy" still produces sufficient lift to serve as a flotation aid in an emergency.

EXTREMELY WELL BUILT

Essentially, the small inflatable boats consist of a floor and an air-filled external shell, as well as, possibly, a spray skirt and other accessories (e.g. fin, thigh strap, luggage zip). In addition, you usually have an inflatable seat, including backrest, which is plugged into the hull.

If you have groups or pairs, where not all of the members have the confidence to cross a cold mountain lake, the combination of SWACK and packraft has certain benefits. After having ascended to the tarn, the swimmer(s) can cross the body of water swimming, while the other, less hardy or less experienced, group members can use the packraft(s) for the crossing.

Packrafts have also proven their worth many times as safety boats for big wild-swimming groups that are travelling in remote areas. From their elevated position, the person in the boat has a much better overview of the group, which means they can intervene quickly and support a swimmer if needed.

THE PACKRAFT MODELS

Mixed double
The biggest models are designed for two people. If you are going to paddle as a couple or a pair, these boats are much better value, in terms of value for money and also the weight-per-head ratio, than buying two single-person models. If this type of boat is only used by one person, it is possible to carry higher payloads and, in still water, even bicycles! On average, this type of boat has a weight of approx. 3.5kg. Of this type, I use an Anfibio Sigma TXV.

Ultralight
It is hard to believe, but the lightest boat model on the market today only weighs about 800g (Anfibio Nano SL). Of course, this model is not suitable for big payloads, long distances or whitewater. However, you can use it for sailing on or crossing rivers, lakes, coves or fjords. If the intention is to carry the boat equipment in SWACKs or swim buoys, then these boats are an ideal choice. Of this type, I use an Anfibio Alpha XC.

LIGHTWEIGHT? YES! EASILY DAMAGED? NO!

Naturally, the lightweight and thin material of the boat brings up the question of how robust it is. It is important to note that the skin of a packraft is nothing like that of cheap PVC dinghies that you can buy in a supermarket. Real packrafts are made of urethane-coated nylon. Due to a special surface treatment, this material is extremely robust as well as being resistant to cold temperatures and UV radiation.

Performance
Depending on the model and equipment level, these boat types have a more robust external skin as well as additional spray skirts and thigh straps. As a result, they are suitable for whitewater, the high seas and, in the hands of experts, even for Eskimo rolling. These boats weigh approx. 3kg. Of this type, I use an MRS Alligator 2S Pro.

SPECIAL EDITIONS

Some models are available as special editions with air-tight and water-tight zips (Internal Storage System/ ISS or TubeBags). In this way, luggage can be stored inside the air bulge. Meanwhile, the Anfibio Sigma TXV "cargo boat" has a different special feature: its floor has a transparent "window" for watching the underwater world.

Paddles are available from ultralight and compact to whitewater varieties. Depending on your preference, the boats can be paddled with a single-bladed (canoe) paddle or a double-bladed paddle.

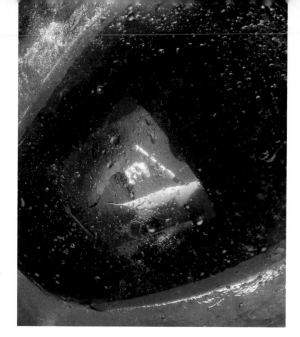

YOUR RELIABLE PACKRAFTING PARTNER

The team of the German company Anfibio Packrafting Stores, with shops in the cities of Dresden and Leipzig, as well as operating an online shop, are competent, outdoor-minded and service-focussed. They don't just sell the best packrafts on the market but also have their own development and maintenance departments and are true professionals with a passion for packrafting!

CONTACT

Anfibio Packrafting Store
Leipzig I Dresden
Tel: 0049 341 3928 1264
info@packrafting-store.de
www.packrafting-store.de
www.packrafting.de (blog)

HANSJÖRG RANSMAYR'S
"FEELING FOR WATER"

"The whole-body water sommelier"

When performance swimmers talk of a "feeling for water", they mean their sense of getting a better grip on the water in order to achieve increased propulsion, thereby swimming faster. To Hansjörg Ransmayr, this definition is rather one-dimensional. To him, a "feeling for water" means much more. It describes a holistic way of feeling, tasting and sensing the element in which you are currently moving, and what it does with or to you.

A holistic definition of this kind is needed because, in contrast to the standardised, chlorinated, dead water of a swimming pool, the water that one encounters in a "wild" body of water is always new, always different and always exciting. Even if you swam in the same pond or pool day in, day out, you would find this to be the case.

This is because the temperature, wind, sunlight, rain, fallen leaves, currents and mineral content are continuously creating new "flavours". Smelling, tasting,

grasping and sensing the water all help to develop a feeling for it, so that, over time, one becomes able to distinguish extremely fine nuances – on your skin and in your nose, mouth and soul. This applies, in particular, if one spends one's life exploring many different waters and temperature ranges. Water can expand our sensory horizon. When we surrender to the fascination of weightlessness, diving into the silence, into the intent to find our own rhythm, then many of our worries and burdens can "dissolve" in the water.

In his wild youth, Hansjörg was an enthusiastic alpinae kayaker. During those early years, he had already swum in the cold alpine waters, sometimes voluntarily and at other times less so, when the power of the whitewater proved stronger than him and his boat! It was only a small step from there to the open water. And it was the open-water swimming where the man from Salzburg earned his first stripes in salt water. He was the first Austrian

to swim the Strait of Gibraltar, and he managed to cross the ice-cold water from the prison island of Alcatraz to San Francisco "by fair means". In 2010, he was the first and only Austrian to participate in the Winter Swimming World Championships in the freezing water of Lake Bled. Being a man of the mountains and a keen mountain hiker, it was only logical that Hansjörg soon discovered his love of native mountain lakes and wild water. He founded the Facebook group Wildswimming World and the info blog alpine-swimming.com. With these online activities, he also employs his many abilities honed during his decades-long career as Creative Director of an advertising agency. He has written several books on wild swimming and works as a freelance concept developer, copywriter and author.

Hansjörg is also involved in various TV and film projects on topics around wild, alpine and ice swimming. Under the slogan "Swimsalabim", a play on a German word

suggesting a magical instantaneous occurrence, he creates events and swimming projects for tourist associations. He also consults mountain cableway/railway operators concerning the utilisation of water collection ponds for snow cannons during the summer months. In addition, he offers guided tours and travel in the sector of swim hiking, swim adventure and swim enjoyment. As a certified mountain hiking guide and active lifeguard, he is particularly interested in the topic of safety by and in the water. This is one of the reasons why Hansjörg is heavily involved in the development of innovative products, such as the SWACK, for use in open-water swimming. Furthermore, he is a core member of both the Austrian and international open-water and ice-swimming community.

Wild Swimming
Croatia and Slovenia
Discover the most beautiful springs, rivers, waterfalls, lakes and beaches in Croatia and Slovenia

Text
Hansjörg Ransmayr

Editor
Katharina Theml, Büro Z, Wiesbaden, Germany

Editor
Thomas Moser

Design
Margaret Prepasser

Typesetting & proofreading
Patrick Davies

First published in German by
Haffmans Tolkemitt, April 2021

This edition published by
Wild Things Publishing Ltd.
Freshford, Bath, BA2 7WG

Distribution
Central Books Ltd
50, Freshwater Road
Dagenham, RM8 1RX
020 8525 8800
orders@centralbooks.com

Contact:
hello@
wildthingspublishing.com

Other books from Wild Things Publishing